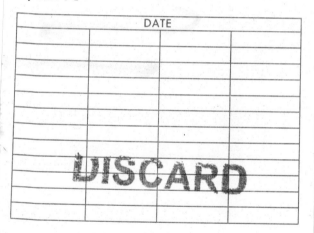

DATE			
	DISCARD		

Developmental Issues in Small Island Economies

Developmental Issues in Small Island Economies

DAVID L. McKEE
&
CLEM TISDELL

PRAEGER

New York
Westport, Connecticut
London

Library of Congress Cataloging-in-Publication Data

McKee, David L.
Developmental issues in small island economies / David L. McKee
and Clem Tisdell.
p.   cm.
Includes bibliographical references.
ISBN 0-275-93393-8 (alk. paper)
1. Caribbean Area—Economic policy. 2. Economic development—
Environmental aspects—Caribbean Area. 3. Oceania—Economic
policy. 4. Economic development—Environmental aspects—Oceania.
5. Caribbean Area—Industries. 6. Oceania—Industries.
7. Caribbean Area—Population. 8. Oceania—Population.
I. Tisdell, C. A. (Clement Allan) II. Title
HC151.M39   1990
338.99—dc20   90-31967

Library of Congress Catalog Card Number: 90-31967
ISBN: 0-275-93393-8

First published in 1990

Praeger Publishers, One Madison Avenue, New York, NY 10010
An imprint of Greenwood Publishing Group, Inc.

Printed in the United States of America

The paper used in this book complies with the Permanent
Paper Standard issued by the National Information Standards
Organization (Z39.48–1984).

10 9 8 7 6 5 4 3 2 1

Contents

Acknowledgments

From the inception of the current project the authors, singly or in consort, have benefitted from the input or support of various colleagues. Included are Te'o Ian Fairbairn, Bernard A. Kemp, James McMaster, Priyatosh Maitra, J. Hans Overbeek, Ransford W. Palmer, R. Sathiendrakumar, and Tjoa Sori-Hock.

In addition Dr. Robert Kiste, Director of the Center for Pacific Island Studies, and Dr. Michael P. Hamnett, Coordinator of the Center for Development Studies, both of the University of Hawaii, Manoa, provided very useful information. Added assistance and information was provided by Dr. Lane Kelley, Director of the Pacific Asian Management Institute, and Angela L. Williams, Director of the Pacific Business Center Program, at the same institution. Jerry B. Norris, Executive Director of the Pacific Basin Development Council, and Gordon Tubbs, of U.S. AID, also provided very helpful information.

The work of preparing the manuscript was simplified substantially through typing, editorial, and research assistance garnered by the authors through their respective institutions. At the University of Queensland, Deborah Ford made major contributions to the typing of the manuscript, and Carunia Firdausy provided helpful research assistance. At Kent State University, Linda Poje was of major assistance in the final editing and typing of the manuscript, as well as seeing it through its various drafts. The Research Council at Kent State supplied substantial travel assistance during the project.

Of course, the authors have no one but themselves to thank for any inadequacies that may be found in the final product.

An Introductory Overview

Among emerging nations, population pressures and problems related to labor absorption are often near the top of the list of issues that must be addressed if the nations in question are to succeed in modernizing their economies and improving the material status of their residents. Rising population surpluses in rural areas, resulting in rural to urban migrations and burgeoning metropolitan squatter settlements, have cast suspicion on population itself as a major villain in the problems of development in Third World nations.

Adding to that suspicion has been the very visible and widely discussed plight of the larger nations among those considered to be poor. The reemergence of interest in China among development specialists, coupled with ongoing difficulties in India, Pakistan, and various other larger Third World nations, has ensured a continuing interest in population as one of the ongoing problems facing developmental processes.

Although there can be no serious counterarguments to the problem status of population in the Third World developmental mix, a cautionary note may be in order. To the extent that population is used as a measure of comparative size, the fact that nations or territories of various sizes can suffer from population problems is obscured. Indeed, in a relative sense, population-related difficulties may be more severe in small jurisdictions.

In such jurisdictions, size itself is a critical problem. Smaller nations may not be able to feed themselves and may not have the domestic market potential to practice import substitution. Thus they are faced with both labor absorption and foreign exchange problems that must be addressed if development is to proceed. Such nations may lack the funds for needed public services and may be unable to provide a basic infrastructure. They may lack natural resources or may be unable to utilize what they have. Their potential for economic diversification is severely limited. They may have difficulties in the management of their monetary sectors, thus exposing themselves to the exigencies of foreign influences. In a relative sense they tend to be far more dependent upon events in the international economy and/or modern nations than are larger Third World nations. Thus it would appear that smaller Third World nations face a cadre of problems that are further complicated by their size, any or all of which may contribute to obstructing their development.

Smallness is more typical of Third World nations than might generally be expected. Recent data indicate that more than 70 Third World nations have populations below the 10 million mark and that 7 more are in the 10 million range. Of those below 10 million, 36 are on the African continent, 22 are in Latin America, and the remainder can be found in Asia, Oceania, and Europe. Thus smallness can be seen to be a worldwide phenomenon. Despite that fact, the small nations in question do not form a homogeneous group that can be studied, as such, in hopes of arriving at prescriptions the planners can administer to many or all of them to speed them on their way toward development.

The current volume does not concern itself with smaller Third World nations in general. Rather, it concentrates upon a particular subgroup of those nations that may have certain unique issues to deal with beyond those appearing to be more generally prevalent among smaller jurisdictions. The subset of nations in question is islands. Among the small island nations (SINs) of the world, the discussion is limited to two geographical groupings — the islands of the Caribbean region and those of the South Pacific.[1]

It is hoped that this discussion of small island concerns against the backdrop of the selected regional groupings will give a good understanding of various developmental problems facing such small economies. The regional groupings selected embrace jurisdictions with a diversity of cultural, social, and political backgrounds and linkages, which undoubtedly have a bearing upon current economic realities.

In the Caribbean region, although domestic cultures are largely extinct, British, Dutch, French, and Spanish influences, not to mention those of the United States, would appear to ensure a diversity of experiences contributing to developmental equations. The region embraces 15 independent states as well as various islands still linked politically in some fashion to Britain, France, the Netherlands, and the United States. In the South Pacific, or perhaps more accurately Oceania, the islands of concern form three regional subgroupings. Micronesia encompasses the area mainly north of the equator and west of the date line. Melanesia covers the region south of the equator and west of the date line. The third subregion is known as Polynesia.

Unlike the Caribbean, Oceania has retained many indigenous cultures of peoples that predate any colonial experiences. "The Pacific island peoples were the last in the world to be colonized" (Meller, 1987, 111). However, during the nineteenth century, various European powers acquired interests in the region. Today many independent small island states have emerged throughout the area, and those jurisdictions are of more interest within the context of the current discussion than are the territories that still retain political linkages of one sort or another with more developed nations.

The approach to be taken will not follow a taxonomy of small island economies and their problems. No developmental formula will be applied on an island-by-island basis, largely because any such formula would appear to be impractical when applied to such a diverse group of economies. Instead, an issue-oriented approach has been adopted with evidence and/or experience which is island specific utilized to set the emphasis. Even among possible issues for discussion, the approach has been selective.

The fact that specific areas of issues have not been included should not be regarded as an implicit suggestion of their unimportance. For example, mainly macroeconomic issues are not discussed. The same is true of monetary concerns and those related to the functioning of the international financial sector. Some of those matters have been well treated by other investigators (Worrell, 1987; Holmes, 1987; and Worrell and Bourne, 1989).

In selecting issues for discussion, attention has been focused upon three main areas of concern. The first set of concerns discussed relates to structural and employment issues. Following that a selection of demographic and socioeconomic issues is reviewed. In the third main section of the book, the emphasis is on environmental and natural resource considerations.

Among the structural issues discussed is the role of staple exports in the economic well-being of SINs. Trade in staple commodities was one of the major forces behind the development of the colonial systems, which lasted well into the middle of the twentieth century. By and large, the history of the Caribbean region was replete with the development of plantation-based economies. Although plantations were later in emerging and much less widespread among the islands of the Pacific, they were a factor in certain jurisdictions. Today, with the terms of trade much less favorable toward staple commodities, economies developed upon such a base are experiencing serious difficulties. Their problems as they relate to small island economies is the preserve of Chapter 1.

Having dealt with primary activity in a small island setting, it seems logical to move on to the role of the secondary sector in those economies. That task is addressed in Chapter 2. Specifically, manufacturing for export as a developmental option is discussed. The strengths and weaknesses of that option, which may be specific to small island economies, are considered. In that context, special emphasis is placed upon how the needs of an export-oriented infrastructure impact expansionary processes. The role of the multinational corporations is also introduced with special emphasis on the developmental impact of decision-making processes within such firms.

In Chapter 3 the emphasis switches to private service activities. The service sector is sometimes viewed as less desirable than manufacturing on the work lists of those concerned with the continuing strength and viability of advanced economies. Without ignoring that debate, the possible role of service activities in small island economies is examined. Special emphasis is placed upon the role of services as facilitators of other types of activity, both domestic and international.

No sectoral analysis of the development potential of any economy would be complete without reference to government activity. Chapter 4 is devoted to assessing the role of the public sector. Specifically, the issue of public service employment is addressed with special reference to how it relates to development.

Many of the island economies in question have placed a major emphasis upon international tourism as a vehicle for development. There is no question that many have much to offer potential tourists. What the tourists themselves may contribute to the welfare of their hosts may be less obvious or definite. In Chapter 5, some of the potential difficulties related to tourism in island ministates are considered.

With Chapter 6 the emphasis switches from structural issues to more people-related problems. More specifically, the role of urbanization in the development process is addressed. Among small island economies urban expansion has become a major factor in developmental patterns. The way in which that process contributes to both centralization and foreign linkages is considered.

As mentioned earlier in the current discussion, population problems are not the unfortunate preserve of very large nations. Indeed, nations of any size may encounter them. Among small island economies, population pressure has the potential for short-circuiting development programs. One of the historical solutions for surplus population in small island states has been out migration. Chapter 7 assesses the developmental implications of migration from and between SINs.

Continuing in a related vein, Chapter 8 discusses issues related to the brain drain and education in general. Specifically, the necessity for educational systems to be responsive to the needs of the jurisdictions concerned is discussed. The positive and negative impacts of the brain drain are outlined. In addition, an effort is made to point out the potential difficulties inherent in assuming that the educational needs of island ministates are parallel to those of larger, wealthier nations.

An aspect of development that appears to have received little attention by economists is the part played by criminal activity. Chapter 9 addresses issues relating to crime as they pertain to the small island economies under discussion. Specifically, the discussion attempts to assess how crime should be regarded by policy makers responsible for allocating funds and other resources. An attempt is made to set priorities with respect to what kinds of criminal activity should receive those allocations within the overall context of developmental needs.

With Chapter 10 the emphasis switches from people-oriented issues to concerns related to agriculture. In a sense, this chapter is a companion piece to Chapter 1, which was concerned with the production of staples for export. Chapter 10 contains a more general treatment of agricultural issues. In essence it attempts to assess the actual role of agriculture in the development of the small island economies concerned.

What Chapter 10 does for the agricultural sector is repeated in Chapter 11 for natural resources. In that regard, fisheries, forest resources, and minerals are considered. Those resources are much more significant among the Pacific economies in question than for those in the Caribbean region. Thus the discussion is largely devoted to Pacific experience.

Chapter 12 completes the discussion of environmental and natural resource issues. In it, environmental and conservation considerations are covered. Here special attention is given to the ecosystems of the small islands in question. Attention is given to pollution as well as to the depletion of various living resources.

In the fourth main section of the volume, the issues presented previously are drawn together in two chapters designed to summarize and unify what has been discussed. In that section, Chapter 13 deals with a selection of international considerations in some detail, and Chapter 14 summarizes the volume and outlines the policy implications of what has been written.

In putting this volume together, the authors have been selective with respect to the issues included. No pretense has been made of presenting the definitive word on all the economic problems facing small island jurisdictions. Nonetheless, within the confines of the issues selected and the regions explored, the aim is to present a realistic appraisal that may be useful for public policy and developmental planning.

NOTE

1. Benjamin Higgins is probably responsible for coining the term SINs (Higgins, 1983).

I

Structural and Employment Issues

1

The Impact of the Primary Export Sector

Economists have been aware for some time of the linkages that exist between the developed world and the economically less fortunate nations of the Third World. The dependency theorists have developed a body of literature that has been extremely critical of the advanced nations with respect to such linkages (e.g., Frank, 1967; 1979). In general their thesis suggests that Third World economies are little more than appendages of the stronger economies and as such are being subjected to continuing forms of exploitation, which can lead only to ongoing and perhaps worsening poverty. In the ideology of the dependency theorists, this situation may bring about a type of development or change in the Third World that actually removes the potential for the type of change that has been at the root of improving circumstances in more fortunate parts of the globe.

Without sharing the ideological bent of the dependency theorists, it seems safe to suggest that there have been some negative symbiotics between the developed nations and the territories that have come to be identified as the Third World. Many of those territories have emerged as independent nations in the second half of the twentieth century. In many cases it seems clear that the economies these fledgling nations have inherited were not designed with an eye to encouraging the integration of activity within their boundaries (McKee, 1977).

The lack of internal integration is evident in various territories that, before their independence, were controlled by European nations. The role of such territories in those economic arrangements was facilitated in many cases by the construction of infrastructures designed to accommodate the needs of what are now foreign interests. Political independence has hardly signalled a rapid adjustment of the infrastructures of Third World nations to domestic needs. Indeed in many cases forces at work in the international economy have further encouraged the enhancement of outward-looking infrastructures, which may or may not be supportive of the overall developmental needs of the nations concerned.

The current authors are concerned with the impact that such circumstances have had and may still be having upon infrastructures and thus development in small island economies. Such impacts with respect to the Third World in general have been of interest to economists for some time. However general impressions garnered from observations involving larger Third World nations may require some fine tuning if they are to be applied successfully to small island jurisdictions. Using practical examples from the Caribbean Basin region and the South Pacific, the current discussion will attempt to supply the above mentioned fine tuning necessary for an understanding of how outward-looking infrastructures are influencing developmental patterns in SINs.

One of the earliest causes of continuing economic contact between various Western European nations and less developed parts of the world was the need for staple commodities. Historians have recognized that one of the most important factors bringing explorers to the Western Hemisphere was the search for a shorter sea route to the Orient to facilitate the procurement of spices and gemstones. The role played by the North Atlantic fishery in the early settlement of Newfoundland has been well documented (Innis, 1954), as has the role of the fur trade in the expansion of settlements in what is today mainland Canada (Innis, 1956).

Both Canada and the United States owe much to the demand for staples in the opening of their interiors. The same can be said for Brazil and various other Latin American nations. The slave economies of the southern United States and the Caribbean Basin were built upon the foundation of plantation agriculture, once again highlighting the importance of staples for export in the processes of development.

With respect to the United States, it has been suggested that regional economies have developed around the processing and export of staples (North, 1970). It seems certain that such expansion brought with it the development of infrastructures designed expressly with the needs of export staples in mind. In areas where this occurred, the nature and positioning of the infrastructures in question undoubtedly have continuing impacts upon the development potential of the regions concerned, long after the particular staples, which may have spawned them, have lost their importance. This may well be the case wherever staples have dictated infrastructure construction, especially with respect to large continental countries. Whether such infrastructures and their impacts have been good or bad in specific cases depends upon the continuing reliability of staple exports and the general utility of the infrastructures and settlement patterns dictated by staples in the past.

Aside from the physical inflexibilities infrastructures can impose upon economies, problems relating to installation and operating costs are never far from the surface. Writing in 1980 Jean Crusol suggested that public expenditures related to infrastructure were running above 20% of government outlays in a selection of Caribbean locations (Crusol, 1980, 57). Such outlays accounted for 42% of government outlays in Trinidad during the period, 1969–1973, and 24% and 25% of public expenditures in Martinique and Guadeloupe between 1971 and 1975 (Crusol, 1980, 57). Obviously once infrastructure facilities are in place, their maintenance and/or improvement will require continuing outlays. SINs typically will not enjoy the luxury of abandoning staple-related infrastructures should staples become less central to their economies. Instead it is more probable that they will have no choice but to make do with such facilities and thus continue the variable cost incurred in their upkeep because the cost of replacement or adjustment may be prohibitive.

No purpose would be served by a general review of the recent performance of staples in world markets. Suffice it to say that the halcyon days of staple exports have long since ended and that this century has seen the terms of trade turning against them (Nurkse, 1967). Thus nations that must rely upon staples to procure manufactured goods in world markets have found themselves increasingly disadvantaged. The need to deliver increasing quantities of staple commodities for export prompts increasing attention to an export-oriented infrastructure.

Historically staple enterprises were rarely designed with the needs of the host territory in mind. Their export was an activity designed to benefit the exporter and the recipient nation (McKee, 1977). The general scenario is well understood by economists. In nations with domestic market potential, the most obvious counterweight to excessive reliance upon staples is import substitution. Where such a strategy is feasible, adjustments in infrastructure may be required. The immobilities engendered in the economy by the existing infrastructure are of course additional encumbrances in the way of development.

In theory the remedies for Third World economies with infrastructures overbalanced toward the needs of staple exports seem clear. Whether such remedies can actually be effectuated remains to be seen. Certainly in the case of SINs, the issue requires further refining. In the Caribbean Basin many small nations owe their current settlement patterns and domestic infrastructures to the dictates of plantation agriculture. The plantation economies of the world include a majority of the islands of the

Caribbean. The list includes all of the Greater Antilles as well as Antigua, Barbados, Dominica, Grenada, Guadeloupe, Martinique, St. Kitts, St. Lucia, St. Vincent, and Trinidad (Beckford, 1983, 14).

In several important respects the historical experiences of island nations in the Pacific differ from those in the Caribbean. European acquisition or domination of Pacific island countries occurred at a much later time (200 or more years later) than in the Caribbean, if we exclude the Southeast Asian countries (Indonesia, the former Dutch East Indies, the Philippines, and Malaya). Although Europeans established plantations in Melanesia, Micronesia, and Polynesia, they were not on such a widespread scale as in the West Indies, and in many Pacific countries traditional economic subsistence activity remained dominant. Local populations were not destroyed as in the West Indies. Tribal, clan, and village social structures survived to a considerable extent in the Pacific and are still a significant factor in the social and political structure of many South Pacific island countries today. For example, a suggested factor in the overthrow of the Labor Government of Dr. Timothy Bavendra in Fiji in the late 1980s (by Rambuka) was the aim of strengthening the power of traditional Fiji chiefs, the desire of tribal groups from the east of Fiji, especially the Lau group, to reassert their dominance in government as well as to avoid possible Indian domination. Timothy Bavendra in contrast to Rambuka is a Fijian from the west, and tribal groups from there have had a long period of conflict with those in the east. To some, especially Fijians from the east, it appeared that the western tribal groups had formed a political association with the Indians in order to gain political power. Despite the continued existence of tribal affiliations in the South Pacific, it, unlike Africa, has been free of major intertribal warfare.

While the European powers, especially Germany, made considerable efforts to establish plantation economies in the South Pacific, they failed to transform fully the countries concerned and had a much smaller impact on them than in the West Indies for several reasons. First, the period of colonial involvement was much shorter in the South Pacific than in the West Indies. Second, slavery had been abolished by the time of European and later U.S. and Japanese involvement in the Pacific islands. This meant that the colonial powers found it more difficult to obtain cheap labor for plantation work. This retarded the rate of plantation expansion. Also, there was no import labor from Africa.

Because the Europeans had abolished slave labor, the European powers turned to the use of indentured labor to operate plantations in the South Pacific. Britain, for example, brought indentured labor from India to Fiji to work on sugar cane and coconut plantations. Indentured labor from one part of the Pacific was frequently engaged to work in another area or country. But such contracts were short-term, e.g., for 3 to 5 years, and islanders were usually repatriated at the end of their contract. Only in the case of the Indians and a small number of Chinese was there noticeable permanent migration, principally to Fiji.

This could have been different if Britain had permitted Germany access to indentured Indian and Chinese labor sources in India, Singapore, and Hong Kong. Although Germany was interested in this option, Britain went to some lengths to deny this source to Germany so as to assist Britain's competitive position relative to Germany. Although there was undoubted commercial rivalry between the colonial powers, British annexations in the South Pacific were largely at the behest of British settlers on the fringes of its empire rather than a calculated economic strategy emanating from Britain itself (Firth, 1986, 7–8). Some economic overtones were present, but they were not Britain's dominant motive.

This contrasted with Germany, which was late by European standards in acquiring colonies. At the start of 1884, Germany was without colonies. By the end of the following year, it had colonies in Togo, Cameroun, East Africa, South-West Africa, New Guinea, and the Marshall Islands. This was "because Bismarck made a decision in principle that Germany was to become a colonial power, a decision dictated primarily by the metropolitan advantages that Bismarck expected would follow" (Firth, 1986, 128). These advantages were seen principally in economic terms, and Germany made strenuous efforts to establish its colonies as a source of raw material, for example, through the establishment of plantations. But Germany's hold over its Pacific colonies was to last for 30 years or less because they were lost during World War I.

But even before its annexation of northeast New Guinea and the Marshall Islands, Germany had extensive commercial interests in the Pacific, chiefly centered on Samoa where, among other things, cotton plantations were established. Firth (1986) argues that Germany's acquisitions in New Guinea were intended to support and complement its involvement in Samoa where its interests were under challenge from the British and Americans.

In any case, it is clear from the above that most island colonies in the Pacific remained colonies for less than 100 years. At least this is true of those acquired by Britain, Australia, and New Zealand. However, France continues to hold its colonies in the Pacific, and the United States has on the whole established special relationships with its territories in that area. But at least for British associated territories, colonial contact was brief, and penetration of economies and societies in the Pacific, incomplete. Indeed, European contact with some tribes in the highlands of New Guinea was not established until the 1950s. As a rule, the first and prime contact of Europeans was with coastal dwellers; contact with inhabitants of the interior of larger Pacific islands was slow in coming. Thus large areas of the Pacific, unlike the West Indies, were not substantially transformed by European contact.

Both world wars had some impact on the Pacific islands whereas they did not affect the Caribbean in a major way. In particular, the Pacific was a major theater of military operations in World War II. This did much to make the indigenous people aware of the outside world and modern technology. World War II also marked a turning point in British colonial policy. After World War II, the view rapidly gained ground in Britain that the nation should divest itself of its colonies as quickly as possible. By the end of the 1970s, Britain and Australia had divested themselves of all colonies in the Pacific.

In former British colonies in the Pacific (more so in some than others), the traditional land and resource rights of the indigenous people have largely been preserved because of the historical developments indicated above. But no such rights remain in the Caribbean. Indeed the indigenous peoples and their cultures have disappeared. One, therefore, has to be very careful in drawing socioeconomic parallels between the Pacific islands and those in the Caribbean.

Of course plantation crops are not alone among primary products in the Caribbean. The oil industry is quite prominent in the region. Although only Barbados and Trinidad and Tobago actually produce crude oil and natural gas (Barry et al., 1984, 88), refining and transshipment facilities are quite common throughout the region. They range in size from a small operation on Barbados, capable of producing 4,000 barrels per day, to what has been cited as the world's largest refinery, situated on St. Croix in the U.S. Virgin Islands (Barry et al., 1984). In addition to those two facilities, refineries exist in Antigua, Aruba, the Bahamas, Cuba, the Dominican Republic, Jamaica, Martinique, Puerto Rico, and Trinidad. Transshipment, bunkerage, and/or distribution facilities can be found in the Bahamas, the Netherlands Antilles, Puerto Rico, and St. Lucia.

Oil is an extractive industry and as such suffers from various uncertainties in world markets. Mexico and Venezuela are textbook cases of what can happen to nations that place too much reliance upon oil and similar industries as a basis for economic growth. Both of those nations mortgaged their futures to develop infrastructure and production facilities to access the supply side of the international market for petroleum products. With oil reserves as a safe form of collateral, the strategy appeared sound until the oil glut of the 1980s.

The islands that house the refining and transshipment facilities cited above have also been affected by changing world market conditions, but that particular set of issues would be better housed in a discussion of industrial development. With respect to the islands that are actually producers, "Barbados does not produce enough petroleum to cover its own needs" (Barry et al., 1984, 88), and even Trinidad is in a relatively weak competitive position (Crusol, 1980, 156). Its wells were dispersed, and pressure is weak, making recovery costly. When these factors are considered in conjunction with modest known reserves, oil from Trinidad is hardly a threat to larger producers (Crusol, 1980, 156).

Despite Trinidad's tenuous position as an oil producer, the activity has occupied an important place in the island's economy. During the 1970s Trinidad and Tobago became a relatively wealthy nation through oil production (Barry et al., 1984, 90). Unfortunately the turnaround in the fortunes of oil during the 1980s has left the nation's hopes for further oil-based development dashed. Instead Trinidad is now faced with the necessity of competing with larger, more efficient producers. The plight of oil production in Trinidad seems to supply additional support for the contention that primary exports make a questionable foundation for development. The capital-intensive nature of the industry, inflexibilities in its positioning, coupled with rather singular requirements with respect to infrastructure, make it a strong candidate for criticisms leveled against plantations. Aside from not providing a climate for more general economic development, it appears to be becoming a developmental liability.

Mining, too, has played a role in the economic history of the Caribbean Basin region. In this century bauxite has been the most significant mineral export. The difficulties that mineral has been having in world markets have had a major role in recent setbacks experienced by the Jamaican economy (Manley , 1987). In addition to Jamaica, bauxite mining has been a factor in the Dominican Republic and Haiti as well as the U.S. Virgin Islands (Barry et al., 1984). Other mining includes nickel in Cuba and the Dominican Republic and aragonite in the Bahamas (Barry et al., 1984). With respect to Third World development in general, minerals require the same caution that should be applied to the export of other staples that can become depleted. "If the mines run out, the justification for certain settlements ceases, facilities become abandoned and the infrastructure supporting the staple becomes redundant" (McKee, 1977).

In the case of very small islands, unsuitable infrastructures based upon export may be less of an issue. Former British possessions in the

ward Island group, while suffering from the adverse trade position
ir plantation crops, may nonetheless benefit from port facilities that
were put in place with staple exports in mind. In those very small countries, distances are sufficiently short that it is difficult to argue that domestic transportation facilities put in place to service the staples have
resulted in problems relating to economic integration. Certainly in some
cases, mountainous interiors are still relatively inaccessible, but access to
such territories is hardly a major factor limiting development potential.
Thus in some cases at least, one cheer can be allotted to the role of staple
exports in developing sustainable internal and external linkage facilities.

The loudness of that cheer may be mitigated to some extent by negative overspills occasioned by the difficulty of maintaining staple exports
as a vehicle for development. Ironically, continuing balance of trade
difficulties may force more intensive staple production, at times even to
the point where export crops take precedence over domestic food
production. The most obvious result from this may be the removal of
rural survival options and a consequent drift of population toward urban
areas.

On very small islands the urban areas in question may house the
docking facilities through which the export staples pass. With increasing
population pressure in the ports, food imports may have to be increased,
a circumstance that tends to further complicate the trade problems.

Beyond that, urbanization creates a need for relatively large outlays
for social overhead capital, which in turn may preclude the expenditure of
public money for their developmental needs (McKee, 1977). The result
may reinforce regional disparities in welfare levels, which may "increase
the gravitational pull of established urban areas" (McKee, 1977), thus
ensuring the continuation of the spiral of inequality and concentration.

In small island economies, such as many of those in the Eastern
Caribbean, the continuing reliance on staple exports may preclude the
development of productive interisland intercourse. This results from the
need for virtually all the islands in question to maximize their staple
contributions to world markets in search of needed foreign exchange with
which to purchase both capital and consumer goods from the developed
world. In their export endeavors, the islands are virtually in competition
with each other. Such competitive behavior hardly encourages stronger
interisland economic ties.

The need to devote as many resources as possible to staple exports
reduces opportunities to develop trade among themselves. The retardation
of interisland trade also blocks opportunities for the SINs in question to
pursue strategies of import substitution. Such strategies have always been

difficult in smaller Third World nations. Ironically, in the case of the island nations of the Caribbean, the need for import substitution has become especially evident in the food sector. The continuing emphasis upon export-oriented plantation crops, coupled with a disdain among residents for agricultural work, dating from the slave era (Beckford, 1983), has left the region with the need to import food.

When this need for substantial food imports is added to an already precarious trade situation, the structural inadequacies of small economies based upon staple exports become even more apparent. In fact, in the Caribbean a large portion of the balance of payments difficulties being experienced has been attributed to food imports, which include "raw and processed foods, animal feeding stuffs, drink and tobacco, which now stand at close to US $1 billion per annum" (Demas, 1988a, 160). Studies seem to suggest that the most efficient strategy for alleviating this situation would be import substitution on a regionwide basis rather than by individual economies acting independently (Demas, 1988a, 162).

Such a strategy would require major adjustments in current practices. In the very small islands, populations have gravitated toward urban port cities. There is an irony in this because such economies, while relying heavily upon staple exports, are nonetheless becoming small city states. The growth of these port cities, which are admittedly not large by metropolitan standards, creates the need for major outlays for social overhead capital, which in turn adjusts the developmental priorities of the nations concerned because public funds are not unlimited. Thus some SINs are experiencing a phenomenon that has been more apparent in larger Third World nations.

Beginning with the slave era, many small islands in the Caribbean were associated with more advanced economies through staple exports. Those exports introduced the profit motive to the region, and, with the exception of military considerations, staples dictated settlement and land tenure patterns as well as the infrastructure to support those patterns. Today many profit-motivated activities are nonprimary in nature in the SINs of the Caribbean. Nonetheless the needs and influences of the earlier plantation era are still quite visible in settlement patterns and infrastructures throughout the region.

Since the abolition of slavery, a rural strata of subsistence farmers has emerged, often relegated to marginal lands that have remained unattractive to plantation enterprises. Parallel to this development has been the continuing growth of urban populations. Neither the rise of independent farmers nor urbanization has been sufficient to alter the influence of the plantations upon domestic transportation and communications facilities, nor have they been effective in reducing the outward-looking bias so prevalent throughout the region. If anything, additions of modern sector activities in the form of services and manufacturing for export have reinforced foreign linkages and undermined policy thrusts in the direction of domestic and, perhaps, regional economic integration.

Neoclassical economists would refer to the situation that has evolved as dualistic. Generally speaking, economic dualism refers to a circumstance where a modern economy is superimposed in some fashion upon a less advanced system. In the SINs of the Caribbean, what would normally be defined as the modern economy, with its linkages to foreign interests, dates from the slave era because previous populations in the region were virtually obliterated by the European ascendancy. Thus developments related to infrastructure have been designed to support the export function from their inception. Islands where less sophisticated subsistence economies have emerged have been confronted with infrastructures not necessarily suited to their needs.

Depending upon the size of the island in question, such an infrastructure may generate or reinforce regional disparities. In the larger islands this appears to have occurred. The export infrastructure has increased the magnetism of urban complexes and adjusted the pecking order of developmental priorities. This effect can be seen in Jamaica, where Kingston is acquiring the problems of major Third World urban areas, with large squatters settlements and urban unemployment, while rural poverty is generating more urban migrants.

To some extent similar trends are evident in Port Moresby, Papua New Guinea, and in Suva, Fiji. Especially in Port Moresby crime is on the increase, and stealing, especially from expatriates and visitors, has become a problem.

The Bahamas presents an unusual variation on the general issue. A small number of islands in that archipelagic nation have had experience with plantation activities. However, the soils were barely suitable, and many export-oriented agricultural ventures have failed. The infrastructure designed to transport the staples seems to have contributed very little to the overall development of the islands in questions. The result has been the migration of population to Nassau and to a lesser extent to Freeport. This migration has of course contributed to urban problems, particularly in Nassau.

If the export-oriented infrastructure generates a widening gap between modern and subsistence pursuits, the result may appear in a lack of island or nationwide economic integration, which of course slows the absorption of labor into the modern sector. On the policy level, import substitution in foodstuffs, which should be feasible through interisland cooperation (Demas, 1988a), seems to be indicated. A major obstacle to such a policy is of course the hold plantations still enjoy on the economies concerned. It is very diffficult to generate food production for domestic or regional markets if such a practice is relegated to marginal lands (see Beckford, 1983). The governments of the islands concerned must play an active policy role. There is no reason why some plantation acreage cannot be relegated to domestic and/or interisland markets. It may well be that such a change in direction may actually remove some of the uncertainties that have plagued the agricultural sector. Unfortunately, official attitudes have been seen as an obstacle to such an adjustment (Crusol, 1980, 122). If the adjustment can be made, it may bring with it a lessening of some of the developmental anachronisms that have been the subject of this discussion.

2

Issues Relating to the Manufacturing Sector

Some of the difficulties associated with the reliance of SINs upon staple exports as a foundation for economic development stem from the questionable position such commodities hold in external markets. If too much reliance upon staple production appears to ensure a weakening or tenuous trading position, an overbalanced domestic infrastructure, and perhaps an increasing need to import food, then it is hardly surprising when those concerned with developmental planning look beyond the staple for the means to support development. In that search, manufacturing for export often emerges as a seductive option. The strengths and weaknesses of that option for SINs is the focus of the current discussion. Special emphasis will be placed upon how the needs of an export infrastructure affect overall development. The impact of decision-making procedures within multinational corporations will also be considered, as will the participation of such firms in import substitution. The discussion will be reinforced by real world references to the small economies of the Caribbean Basin region and the South Pacific.

Recent history is replete with successful manufacturing incursions into world markets by firms and/or production units that are based in Third World nations. Perhaps the most talked of sorties of this type have emanated from Asia where Hong Kong, Singapore, South Korea, and Taiwan have become major success stories. Known as the Four Tigers, these jurisdictions have become major players in world markets. In South America, Brazil has emerged as an influential industrial power. Such successes have hardly gone unnoticed in Third World nations striving to improve their economic performance. In fact manufacturing success, while producing certain obvious benefits, may often obscure serious ongoing economic difficulties.

Economists have known for some time that modernization based upon export-oriented manufacturing may generate an outward-looking infrastructure (McKee, 1977). Such production facilities will have a tendency to locate in areas that give them ready access to the world economy and/or foreign markets. Thus urban areas functioning as seaports will enjoy a definite advantage over inland cities. In larger Third World countries, the emphasis on export may generate difficulties with respect to economic integration at the national level. The need to provide state-of-the-art export linkages may tax public expenditure priorities to such an extent that integrative infrastructure facilities may go begging.

Speaking of Caribbean microstates, DeLisle Worrell cited infrastructure improvements as "a major prerequisite for growth" (Worrell, 1987, 166). Among his wish list were well-equipped airports to facilitate tourism, new roads for agricultural purposes, port facilities for commodity shipment as well as reliable utilities. Worrell was speaking of the very smallest of Caribbean economies. In the case of the small nations of the Caribbean in general, it would appear as though improvements in the technology of transportation and communications, coupled with the proximity of the mass markets of the North American mainland, would tend to encourage the development of export-oriented manufacturing activities.

In small island economies the potential for economic problems of a developmental nature, stemming from the need for an export-oriented infrastructure, may seem to be less worrisome than has been the case in larger Third World nations. To begin with, the very smallness of many of the islands in question may mean that the financial demands of a domestic infrastructure are modest and in many cases may be co-extensive with the demands of the export sector. However, what may seem modest in comparison to the needs of larger nations may be substantial in terms of the ability of small island economies to afford them.

The impact of the financial demands of an export-oriented infrastructure must be examined on a case-by-case basis. Jurisdictions like Barbados or Aruba may be able to meet such demands rather well, but the same may not be true of Jamaica or the Bahamas. In the case of the first two islands cited, it is perhaps true that domestic problems related to distance are minimal, but the same cannot be said of the remaining two economies. In Jamaica the need for an export-oriented infrastructure might very well affect development potential in parts of the country where export activity is not a priority. It is quite conceivable in such economies that outward-looking infrastructures will adversely affect domestic economic integration. The problems of domestic integration may become even more severe in archipelagic nations like the Bahamas if the financial needs of an export infrastructure displace transportation and communications projects to service the domestic economy from developmental priorities.

Even in very small islands, where an outward-looking infrastructure may serve domestic needs well, developmental priorities may have to be altered to secure the financial resources required to complete infrastructure facilities. Barring some form of aid or foreign financing, the construction of airports, harbor facilities, and other export-oriented infrastructure projects may force the postponement of government expenditures on health, education, and other domestic needs. The potential impact of such priority adjustments should be weighed in advance by those concerned with development.

The infrastructure and its impact on overall developmental goals constitutes only one set of issues to be considered if manufacturing for export is to be encouraged in small island economies. Other important considerations revolve around the role of foreign-owned manufacturing firms. The entry of such enterprises into the developmental mix in Third World nations has been recognized by economists as having a potential for difficulties as well as advantages (McKee, 1977). One of the more serious difficulties revolves around "the global basis of decision making which results in the tendency inherent in direct investment from abroad to shift decision-making power in parts of the private sector outside the country" (Parry, 1973). Small island economies are even less well equipped to deal with this scenario than are larger Third World hosts. In many cases the financial statements of the corporations involved outstrip those of host governments, and their global workforces may exceed the total populations of certain island host economies. As has been suggested for host nations in general (Parry, 1973), the national interests of small island economies may be in direct conflict with international corporate concerns.

The implication is not that hosting manufacturing facilities owned by multinational corporations is always questionable for small island economies. Certainly the practice does link such jurisdictions more closely to the world economy, but the utility of such linkages from the point of view of those concerned with development must be assessed on a case-by-case basis. Certainly "international firms are pursuing their own interests and are only peripherally concerned with the welfare of specific countries" (McKee, 1977). Any involvement that such corporations may have with small island economies will reflect their own needs or perceived advantages rather than those of their hosts. This is not to suggest that the intentions of multinational corporations toward small island economies are necessarily negative or suspect. It simply means that those concerned with the development of such economies should keep their general developmental goals in mind as they move to expand corporate activities, especially those involving multinationals.

Once corporate facilities have been implanted, planners need to be able to predict future changes in those facilities. The kind of information that the domestic planners would appear to require unquestionably necessitates close cooperation with the corporate planners. Such cooperation may be difficult to attain, particularly in cases where corporate decisions are made beyond the boundaries of the country in question. Decision making in this mode is thought to pose potential threats to sovereignty through its ability to circumvent domestic economic policy (Parry, 1973).

The strength of small island governments with respect to hosting corporate facilities may be further eroded by the seeming willingness of some governments to make concessions to attract industry. The felt need for export industries, which exists in various Caribbean nations, is undoubtedly known by potential corporate investors. Economists and political leaders in the region have made no secret of their interests. Speaking in 1988 William Demas, the Governor of the Central Bank of Trinidad and Tobago, suggested the need for a much more outward-looking manufacturing sector in the Caribbean: "We have no choice but to produce exports competitively on a large scale for extra-regional markets, whether the products are based on our own local and regional raw materials and other inputs or on those imported from outside the region" (Demas, 1988b, 12).

The type of export-oriented manufacturing sector, which Demas feels is needed, is clearly one in which the nations concerned have some role to play in selecting both the products and their markets. He called for "a more planned and systematic approach to penetrating export markets" and suggested that "efforts have to be well targeted and more product and country-specific" (Demas, 1988b, 13). Citing the successful experience of newly industrialized countries, he declared, "Deliberate state intervention has worked, and continues to work, in harness with local private initiatives" (Demas, 1988b, 13).

Presumably the type of export sector that Demas advocates would ensure some local control of the decision-making processes, thus avoiding some of the pitfalls of international decision making with respect to sovereignty. Whether the small economies in question can actually enter world markets in the manner being advocated remains to be seen; nevertheless, what Demas has said highlights the interests that SINs are developing in the potential for manufacturing exports.

Potential corporate investors are well aware of the felt need on the part of small island economies for export expansion. These investors are also aware that various SINs differ widely in their suitability for contemplated corporate activity. In the Caribbean region alone, there are wide variations in development from island to island. Thus foreign capital may well flow toward more developed economies, which of course will widen the gap between themselves and their less fortunate neighbors (Ramsaran, 1985, 138). "Where a country does not have a locational advantage, or . . . [its] advantage is shared by other . . . states, it may be tempting to offer greater and greater concessions in order to attract investors" (Ramsaran, 1985, 138). If there was any reason for corporate investors to locate in such territories in the first place, such concessions may be unnecessarily burdensome. At the very least they will increase the costs of economies for promoting industrial expansion.

The pitfalls associated with interurban and interregional competition for industrial facilities in advanced nations are well known to economists and planners (Levy, 1981; 1987). It is often dangerous to make theoretical and/or practical comparisons between developed economies and emerging nations, but the current case may be an exception. If granting concessions to attract industry to urban areas or regions in mature economies seems ill-advised, might not similar practices among the SINs of the Caribbean or the South Pacific be equally ill-advised? Levy appears skeptical of such practices in the United States. "When viewed at the regional and national level a great deal of local economic development activity has a zero-sum-game character" (Levy, 1987, 135).

The greater and greater concessions alluded to by Ramsaran translate well into Levy's zero-sum-game. Ramsaran foresaw governments pitted against each other in the Caribbean (Ramsaran, 1985, 138). Among the weapons of competition were included such things as tax holidays, forgiveness of import duties, accelerated depreciation, the provision of industrial sites, and even the repatriation of profits (Ramsaran, 1985, 1 and 139). Clearly cooperation between SINs which are related regionally would appear to be a more effective posture if the aim is to attract foreign corporate investors.

Differences in size and strength, not to mention language and culture, in the Caribbean region have made the form of cooperation cited above difficult to attain. Even among former British Colonies, the success of efforts to integrate economic objectives has been mixed. In the Commonwealth Caribbean, wide variations in economic viability based upon size, location, natural resource base, and degrees of overall development exist.

Foreign-owned corporations may have various objectives in seeking to locate facilities in SINs. They are said to use the Caribbean economies in at least five ways: as a source of raw materials, a location for low-wage assembly industries, a center for offshore banking, a market for their own products, and a market for import substitution industries controlled by them (Barry et al., 1984, 14). Overshadowing the specifics of the interests multinational corporations have developed in the Caribbean Basin is the proximity of the islands to the North American market. That proximity has pushed low-wage assembly operations to the fore in some Caribbean locations, notably Haiti and the Dominican Republic (Barry et al., 1984; Crusol, 1980).

The potential for industrialization based upon import substitution is of course a function of the size of local markets and thus, in the case of the smallest islands, presents an additional argument in favor of economic cooperation. If Barry and his colleagues are correct, such cooperation has been far from strong. "Each island has its own industrial promotion agency that tries to lure foreign companies with promises of profit" (Barry et al., 1984, 64). According to Barry those agencies come bearing gifts for prospective enterprises, gifts that are an expected part of the mix to the firms in question. "Nowadays, a foreign firm probably would not consider a location that did not offer unrestricted remission of profits, tax holidays of ten years or more, duty free imports of machinery and raw material, and training programs for its workers" (Barry et al., 1984, 64–65). If that appraisal is accurate today, then the encouragement of multinational firms in the development mix of small island economies appears fraught with problems. In the Caribbean at least, cooperation among the nations concerned might bring the granting of concessions within reasonable bounds.

Most concessions sought by corporations are aimed at cutting the costs of doing business. This is true of dealings in the developed world as well as in emerging nations. In the developed world, concession requests often surface as the location of a new facility is being planned. However, the desired concessions may be well down the list of factors involved in location decisions. Nonetheless, it is good business for corporate planners to pursue them in the same way that it would be good business to explore other cost-cutting measures. Corporate planners should be expected to follow similar cost-cutting procedures in negotiations aimed at locating facilities in SINs.

In dealing with such corporate behavior, development planners in the prospective host territories should be aware of advantages their location offers the multinationals. In the Caribbean in the case of many small island economies, the location offers proximity to North American markets. Coupled with proximity, they can provide a low-cost, literate labor force, political and financial stability, and dependable legal systems.

What SINs have to gain from corporate facilities is another matter. One of the more obvious gains is in employment. In SINs with a surplus labor problem, corporate activity may provide some relief although that relief may come at the lower end of the wage scale. Another potential benefit may come in the form of needed foreign exchange. If the corporations are producing goods for export, such activity may aid the foreign exchange equation. The extent of that aid will depend upon the local content of exports, the final disposition of the revenues that are generated, and the needs of the corporations themselves for imports.

Manufacturing in the South Pacific island countries is less developed on the whole than in the Caribbean. This is partially because of their greater distance from major international markets, the greater degree to which they are scattered compared to the islands in the Caribbean, the extremely small size of local markets except in Fiji and Papua New Guinea (where they are still small), and the superior competitive position of newly industrializing economies in the Pacific Basin, particularly Southeast Asian economies. The prospects for South Pacific island countries developing a major export-oriented manufacturing sector in the near future appear dim. They do not offer wage advantages over Southeast Asian countries, such as the Philippines; supporting services for manufacturing, including regular shipment possibilities, are less developed; their distance from most major international markets is greater, so transport costs are a problem; the work ethic may be less strong than in parts of Southeast Asia; local markets are smaller than in Southeast Asia; and in some locations the lack of available inputs such as electricity and water can constitute a problem. Except for some input from hydroelectricity in Fiji and Papua New Guinea, South Pacific countries rely on imported fuel for both electricity production and general use.

Taking the above into account, multinational corporations planning to establish manufacturing facilities in low-wage cost countries in the Pacific are likely to have a preference for the Philippines, Malaysia, and Thailand over countries such as Fiji and Papua New Guinea. In fact to the extent that Australian companies engage in offshore manufacturing, much of this activity is carried on in Southeast Asian countries, e.g., in the Philippines. This includes the manufacture of garments to Australian design for the Australian market and manufacture of shoe uppers for the same market. Japan's offshore manufacturing activities in the Pacific are concentrated in South Asian and Southeast Asian economies, and it is engaged in import-replacement manufacture or assembly in Australia and New Zealand, e.g., in automobiles.

The two largest economies in the Southwest Pacific island region are Papua New Guinea and Fiji. But their home markets are too small to support a manufacturing industry of significance, and they have a comparative disadvantage in manufacturing in the international market. The situation is even more difficult for smaller countries. The visible exports of all the South Pacific economies consist mainly of primary products.

In Papua New Guinea, for example, the main manufacturing industries include food processing (processing of local products for the domestic market and export), beverage manufacture (beer and soft drinks), tobacco manufacture (principally from imported tobacco leaf by subsidiaries of the multinational companies W.D. & H.O. Wills and Rothmans of Pall Mall), a limited amount of garment manufacture, sawn timber, joinery and wooden furniture manufacture, printing and publishing, manufacture of simple fabricated metal products, concrete products, and paint, some boat building and assembly, and production of handicrafts. Production of machinery (electrical and nonelectrical) is virtually absent. (For more details see, for example, Hunter, 1985, 79–120.)

The smaller and less resource-rich economies in the Pacific region have even less scope for manufacture. Some, e.g., Tuvalu, are subsistence economies and have very little surplus to process for export, so they have little scope to add value to exports through manufacturing. Even cooperation between small Pacific island countries may fail to overcome the disadvantages their location, small market size, and resource scarcity impose in relation to manufacturing development.

At one time the processing and export of raw materials had been considered a boon to certain island economies. However recent experience in the Caribbean region has cast some doubts upon such activity. Jamaica has suffered economic setbacks in the export of bauxite (Manley, 1987), and various islands have suffered from the depressed state of the world market for petroleum products. Refining facilities that exist in many locations through the Caribbean region have been hard hit by the oil glut. Closures and/or cutbacks have occurred in the Bahamas, Puerto Rico, the U.S. Virgin Islands, the Netherlands Antilles, and Trinidad and Tobago. The last economy listed has been especially hard hit because it was the site of production as well as refining. A reliance upon the processing of raw materials for export would seem to have the same potential for difficulties as was cited for staple commodities in Chapter 1.

In the case of petroleum the problems may be even more severe because changing conditions in world markets may idle large capital facilities. Depending upon the ownership of such facilities, problems associated with closures and cutbacks may be more or less severe. The sheer size of the oil sector may have a devastating impact upon very small economies when it experiences difficulties. Petroleum is the major "economic force in Trinidad and Tobago's economy . . . which tends to determine the pace of overall economic activity" (Ramsaran, 1985, 140). Certainly that particular nation would benefit from the type of interisland cooperation that might ensure a relatively stable regional demand for its petroleum products. Such a scenario may be feasible for Trinidad as foreign oil companies cut production in their Caribbean refineries. Even the economies suffering from such cutbacks would benefit from a stable and potentially cheaper source for their own petroleum needs.

As mentioned earlier, foreign corporations may have an interest in producing for local markets in SINs. The degree of interest is related to the size of those local markets. Thus the poorest and/or smallest of the economies in question will have the least potential for attracting such activity. Once again regional cooperation among SINs may make the location of production facilities of this sort more feasible.

On the surface it would appear that the acquisition of production facilities geared to local markets is desirable. Import substitution has been of interest to development planners in the Third World for some time. In small island economies, with relatively severe foreign exchange and/or balance of payments problems, it would seem that anything able to reduce the long list of import items should be encouraged. However, the overall impact of facilities geared to local markets must be assessed. Such production units will require imports of their own. These will have to be weighed against the impact that production geared to local markets can be expected to have on the importation of similar products, if the actual impact of the new or contemplated facilities is to be assessed. Beyond the foreign exchange aspect of the issue, the impact of the facilities on local labor and resource markets should be estimated.

Writing about Trinidad, Ramsaran appears skeptical of foreign investors with interests in domestic sales (1985, 140). He cites their apparent interest in capturing the local market "by getting behind the high protective 'walls' which government has used to encourage local industry." He was writing about production facilities geared for export that content themselves, once in place, with local business. He suggests that such operations tend to become local monopolies, which in turn adversely affect quality and pricing policies (Ramsaran, 1985, 140). To the extent that his points are well taken additional cautionary notes must be added to those already discussed if facilities run by the multinationals and geared to import substitution are to be encouraged.

By way of summary, small island economies seeking to develop through a strategy of industrialization based upon encouraging the activities of multinational corporations will do well to analyze the potential impact of such industrial implants in advance. Such planning, it is hoped, will minimize the potential difficulties and thus increase the chances for beneficial results.

Matters to do with infrastructure should be high on the investigation list of any impact analysis. On the one hand, corporate facilities that create an outward-looking infrastructure and that, because of costs and/or use of labor and materials, generate high opportunity costs with respect to other developmental needs may be ill-advised. On the other hand, if the infrastructure generated by corporate needs is of a multipurpose nature, perhaps the corporate venture should be accepted.

In encouraging multinational corporations small island economies should pay attention to the future plans of those organizations. It seems advisable to request such information because large production facilities can seriously impact small jurisdictions through their demands upon energy, resources, and the environment. Care should be taken to be selective in accepting corporate projects and to understand the potential of such operations in the international economy. Recent experiences in the Caribbean region, with respect to oil and bauxite, support the wisdom of such a practice.

In weighing the potential benefits from proposed corporate facilities, it would appear that the creation of employment opportunities and the easing of foreign exchange difficulties should be high on the list of items to consider. With respect to both, it would seem that the amount of local content in goods to be produced is very important as are potential markets for the goods in question.

SINs should be realistic in appraising their potential as platforms for export-oriented production. Granting a wide range of concessions to attract firms may be unnecessary in some cases and counterproductive in most cases. Firms that make location decisions based upon such concessions may be less than desirable additions to small island host economies. Competition between small island economies through granting concessions may be as harmful as similar practices that pit local areas against each other in advanced economies. The elimination of such competitive practices is a strong argument for cooperation among small island economies.

Another incentive for such cooperation rests with the potential for import substitution. If small nations reasonably close geographically could cooperate, together they might be able to develop regional markets of sufficient size to generate profitable production opportunities, which in turn might reduce the list of items necessarily purchased from outside the region. Even in the case of multinationals interested in production facilities geared to meet the needs of local markets, care should be taken to minimize monopoly influences on price and product quality, not to mention the potential for blocking local entrants to the manufacturing sector.

Economists have known for some time that in small nations "the opportunity for efficient import-substituting industrialization is exhausted relatively quickly" (Helleiner, 1973), and "there is little possibility of establishing an industrial mix which is not export oriented" (McKee, 1977). It is hoped the present discussion has provided an overview of some of the matters that must be considered by those concerned with developmental policy in small island economies.

3

The Role of the
Private Service Sector

It has been suggested that among Third World nations some countries "are so poor and so bereft of natural resources that they will not demonstrate any significant development for decades to come, if ever" (Herbst, 1988). Included in that cadre of unfortunate nations were "the Sahelian countries of Africa . . . and many of the island nations of the Pacific" (Herbst, 1988). Negative assessments of the development potential of Third World nations have never been popular among politicians. Indeed the term Third World has perhaps obviated the necessity for employing somewhat less palatable terms for nations in the plight described by Herbst.

Among the more obvious reasons for poverty on a national scale are lack of natural resources and difficulties relating to climate and/or topography. Another serious impediment to material progress in many nations has been overpopulation and the many difficulties that condition generates. In the case of the SINs of the Third World, problems of isolation and critical mass may have to be added to some of those listed above.

Issues relating to the production of primary commodities for export have been discussed earlier in the present volume, as have both the problems and potential of manufacturing activity. For small island economies, development based upon primary and secondary activities appears to bring with it various possible pitfalls. That is not to suggest that the jurisdictions in question can never benefit from primary and secondary pursuits. However, the possible difficulties are sufficient to suggest that the tertiary sector must also be examined if any accurate appraisal of the development potential of small island economies is to be achieved. The present chapter will move the discussion in that direction.

Unquestionably some of the smallest of SINs do suffer from the situation described by Herbst. In the Caribbean Basin region, development in some of the smaller islands has lagged behind Barbados and

Trinidad and Tobago. In some cases smallness coupled with inadequate transportation linkages has caused the discrepancy. The prognosis for those smaller islands, based upon primary and secondary activity, seems far from encouraging. Whether or not tertiary or service pursuits can stimulate genuine economic progress in those very small nations remains to be seen.

Services for profit have sometimes been viewed as less desirable than manufacturing, by those concerned with the continuing health and strength of advanced economies (Cohen and Zysman, 1987). "In a Keynesian sense many service endeavors geared towards consumers are perceived by economists to be induced activities, presumably generated in urban areas because of a successful manufacturing base" (McKee, 1988, 112). This view of services if generalized can hardly be expected to generate much enthusiasm among development planners in small island economies. Services of a derivative nature, induced by demands generated from income earned in primary or secondary pursuits may be viewed as far from central to developmental processes. In jurisdictions where manufacturing is minimal and primary pursuits are weak economically, little can be expected from services that rely upon these activities to generate the income needed to make service purchases feasible.

Governments, rather than the private sector, in Southwest Pacific island countries play a relatively larger role in the provision of services than in more developed countries. Services provided by governments include marketing of many agricultural export products (e.g., coffee in Papua New Guinea), research and development services for agriculture and fisheries, education, health services (e.g., public hospitals, police, justice and corrective services), communications (e.g., telecommunications and postal services), and some transport services. Several small Pacific nations have cooperated to form the Forum Shipping Line to supply intercountry shipping services within the Pacific. The public provision of services is discussed in more detail in the next chapter.

Because the manufacturing sector is extremely small, in small island developing countries in this region, it provides little stimulus to the growth of complementary private services. Apart from household demand for private services, government demand appears to be a major influence on the development of the private service sector.

Nevertheless, provision of services by the private sector is far from insubstantial especially in the larger island economies and those with sizable urban centers, e.g., Fiji and Papua New Guinea. Private sector provision of services includes retailing and distribution of goods, supply of tourist services such as hotels and restaurant services, some shipping services, taxis and bus services, legal, accounting, and medical services, banking, and insurance. The range and variety of private services is related to the size of the economy.

Except in the larger urban centers of the Pacific's less developed islands, the residents rely heavily on subsistence products (self-grown or harvested), more so than in the West Indies. To the extent that exchange of village produce takes place, it is largely via village and municipal markets or by roadside selling. But in several urban centers, supermarkets and retail stores along the lines of those in more developed countries are well established and their occurrence is spreading. These food outlets principally sell imported and prepackaged goods and locally "manufactured" food and beverage products. The import content of such retail outlets is very high in contrast with that of produce in traditional markets where it is virtually zero. The trend toward greater reliance on such outlets for provisions is of concern because it places increasing pressure on the balance of payments and makes it more difficult for villagers to market their traditional produce because of switches from it to imported produce sold through retail establishments (B. Hardaker, pers. comm.).

Despite some services being derivative in nature, most advanced economies are service oriented. In 1988 service pursuits were credited with accounting for nearly two-thirds of the GNP in the United States and almost three-fourths of employment (Waite, 1988, 20). Any judgments on the goodness or badness of these realities must be prefaced by a knowledge of the causes of service ascendancy. Beyond the suggestion that service expansion is directly related to urbanization and/or growth in income, various other reasons for the increasing prominence of such activities in advanced economies have been suggested. "Growth in goods production and the increased use of contracting out by these producers has greatly expanded measured service receipts" (Waite, 1988, 20). Waite also refers to demographic and social factors such as an aging population and the women's movement. Last on his list of causal factors was "expansion in computer-based information technology along with deregulation" (Waite, 1988, 21).

Another causative element in service expansion has been the rise of multinational enterprise with its attendant service needs. Today manufacturing operations require a variety of sophisticated services to facilitate their success. "In many manufacturing enterprises, the cost of service inputs now exceeds the cost of production workers by a considerable margin" (Feketekuty, 1988, 8). Feketekuty suggests that improvements in transportation and communications, together with data processing capabilities, "have dramatically reduced the cost and time required to acquire services from distant suppliers, and this has expanded the geographic area within which service inputs are bought and sold" (Feketekuty, 1988, 10). Clearly such services are not simply induced additions to the economies of advanced nations, much less to the world economy. "International business would not be possible without extensive international trade in services" (Feketekuty, 1988, 18).

In the economies of advanced nations, various services related to business have been described as "facilitating agents, in much the same way as a flux operates in the amalgamation of metals" (McKee, 1988, 20). Within manufacturing processes inputs from various service cadres may be unrecognizable, but the processes in question might not have been feasible without the contributions of business and engineering consultants and other service subcontractors (McKee, 1987; 1988). Thus various service pursuits, through their interaction with manufacturing processes, strengthen the influence of those processes upon modern economies, not to mention the international economy. Business-related services have been identified as actual facilitators of change in advanced economies (McKee, 1987; 1988).

If this is true, such services may play that role in the international economy as well. If services that are related to business have become facilitators of change in the world economy, as well as in advanced nations, it is to those service subsectors that one must look in attempting to identify a leadership role for services in Third World expansion. Highly visible, low-skill consumer services tend to obscure the potential of the service sector in Third World settings in much the same way that they have retarded an understanding of service ascendancy in advanced economies.

In Third World settings, however, even menial service pursuits, including some that are housed in the urban informal sector, may provide survival options to some elements of the population, thus perhaps improving the economic status and positioning of those at the base of the income pyramid (McKee, 1988). This is not a ringing endorsement of menial services as an engine for development, but it does suggest that those services, by their mere existence, are far from indicative of stagnation or weakness. They do not exist in Third World settings through the defaulting of labor markets. There may even be an air of optimism among those employed in them. Nevertheless, their existence hardly signals that a nation is on the road to development.

It appears as though the search for the role of services in the development process is far more complicated than might have been anticipated.

"For actual development to progress, the way must be opened for the absorption of labor into modern sector jobs that pay better than subsistence wages" (McKee, 1988, 35). Ironically, changes in the world economy, specifically the nature and positioning of manufacturing facilities, may lead to the needed labor absorption in Third World economies. The irony in the situation comes from the fact that the changes alluded to have been made possible by service innovations or, more specifically, services in the role of facilitators as referred to earlier in this chapter.

"Some countries have developed a reputation for professional excellence in certain areas of engineering, software design, accounting, management consulting, architecture, economic analysis and forecasting, printing, data processing, and advertising" (Feketekuty, 1988, 11). All those activities are examples of facilitative services that operate in the international economy. These service cadres, together with improvements in transportation and communications, have made major contributions to the feasibility of multinational production processes. If manufacturing facilities operated by multinational firms are situated successfully in Third World locations, these services or some combination of them will have played a role.

Various sophisticated services, many of which may not be located in Third World nations, are contributing to the feasibility of production facilities in those nations. Certain problems related to manufacturing endeavors in small island economies have been alluded to in the preceding chapter. Those problems notwithstanding, it seems safe to say that production facilities, and whatever development opportunities they may make possible in SINs, would be much less practical in the absence of an array of sophisticated services in the international economy.

Feketekuty goes further than the suggestion that services facilitate international business. To him international business "would not be possible without extensive international trade in services" (Feketekuty, 1988, 18). A somewhat more jaded view of services in the international economy has been put forth by Bennett Harrison and Barry Bluestone. Paraphrasing an argument they attribute to Richard Walker, they suggest that the "growth of services constitutes not so much a fundamental transformation of what capitalism produces as much as a manifestation of how it does it" (Harrison and Bluestone, 1988, 74). They go on to suggest that the service ascendancy was occasioned by the emergence of a more complex technology and the spreading of production among widely separate locations. Further fuel for service needs arises "as businesses need to tend to their relations with more and more governments . . . and as the labor force of multinational corporations must be coordinated and controlled over greater distances, legions of supervisors, . . . repairers, and paper shufflers become an even larger part of day-to-day business" (Harrison and Bluestone, 1988, 74).

Feketekuty's assessment, if less flamboyant, seems no less emphatic: "The service industries provide the transportation, the communications, the financing, the insurance, the know-how, and all the other support systems that are needed for world commerce" (1988, 18). The thrust of the current discussion appears to support the argument that sophisticated business services facilitate manufacturing operations in Third World nations (McKee, 1988). However, it is not clear that many of the services required will actually be located in Third World nations. In many cases the firms supplying such services have emerged as multinationals in their own right and are often head-officed in advanced nations.

Making the point that the emergence of various services has facilitated the industrialization of certain Third World nations may be less than interesting to development planners in small island economies that have no manufacturing activity or where manufacturing may be generating or experiencing some of the problems referred to in the preceding chapter. In jurisdictions experiencing negative externalities from manufacturing, the services that facilitated the offending production units should hardly be expected to be endorsed. Thus sophisticated arrays of facilitating services may run the gamut from being very helpful to being seriously dysfunctional in terms of their impact upon specific small island jurisdictions.

In such nations where no production activity seems feasible, much less helpful to developmental aims, it might appear that there should be no interest in services in the role of facilitators. Events in the world economy have shown that this view may be an oversimplification. "In some cases the facilitating services have become multinational firms in their own right. When that is the case they may even boast branches in Third World nations" (McKee, 1988, 118). The presumed benefit from hosting such activities has been recognized in the Caribbean area. Speaking in Kingston, Jamaica, William Demas specified the need for Caribbean jurisdictions to "seek to maximize . . . foreign exchange earnings from skill-intensive and knowledge-intensive services sold to foreigners" (Demas, 1988b, 14). It is not clear from the context whether Demas was proposing the sale of such services generated by strictly domestic talent or whether he would entertain branches of multinational service firms, provided that such operations could produce the desired results. In any case he was explicit in his shopping list of services, which included "engineering design and consulting, large-scale construction, petroleum and bauxite technology, tertiary-level education and agronomy" — services he proposed to sell to Third World nations (Demas, 1988b, 14). For customers among developed nations, he proposed offshore university education, health, finance, and information processing. All of these activities he felt could help with the foreign exchange problems of the jurisdictions that provided them (Demas, 1988b, 14).

Whether SINs can successfully market the services suggested by Demas to customers in the Third World remains to be seen. India is widely recognized as having been successful in this regard and has been especially successful in marketing its services to less developed African countries. In the South Pacific, the residents of Kiribati are known to be excellent seafarers and are in demand to staff the ships of other nations. This is an important source of income and foreign exchange for Kiribati. According to Feketekuty (1988, 119), international competitiveness with respect to services is determined, among other things, by labor costs together with the knowledge and skills of the local labor force and management.

In the Caribbean region the University of the West Indies, with its three main campuses in Jamaica, Barbados, and Trinidad, is well recognized as a quality institution. Despite that, numbers of English-speaking students from the Caribbean elect to study in Great Britain, Canada, and the United States, thus depriving the nations housing the regional university of potential foreign exchange credits. The support of students in the wealthier nations mentioned constitutes a drain of exchange dollars for the region. Nonetheless, students trained by the regional university may be able to provide their homelands with the skills needed to supply at least some of the services alluded to by Demas. Thus, the university earns exchange dollars directly when it trains foreign students and creates the potential to earn more if its graduates are employed successfully in supplying international services. Of course, the overall impact of the university on exchange requires a knowledge of what must be imported to support its operation. It enhances the labor forces of the nations that house it, and, by keeping talented young people at home for their educational experiences, it may also reduce the ever present threat of the brain drain.

In the Pacific, undergraduate students from former British territories rarely go abroad except to New Zealand, for they are relatively well catered to by the University of the South Pacific with its headquarters in Suva, the University of Papua New Guinea in Port Moresby, and the University of Technology in Lae. Australian government financial support has been directed to assisting with tertiary education *in* the countries concerned. This plus the nature of Australian immigration policy has meant that there has been virtually no brain drain from the Pacific islands to Australia. In the case of New Zealand, however, some brain drain from the islands has occurred.

According to Feketekuty (1988, 119), international competitiveness in services is also affected by the availability of data processing and communications facilities. Throughout the Caribbean there is a wide variation in the availability of such equipment. Many of the smaller and poorer islands have little to offer along these lines. The installation of such equipment in those locations would not ensure that business will be drawn away from wealthier players within the region.

Other matters perceived by Feketekuty to enhance international service competitiveness include "the effective organization of service inputs required to deliver the services desired by customers, the institutional environment for the production of services, and proximity to the market" (1988, 119). Here Feketekuty appears to be alluding to the need for an infrastructure conducive to providing the services he has in mind, as well as an available market for such services. In the Caribbean region, transportation and communications facilities, together with physical positioning, have a major influence upon the potential for international services both to Third World customers and others. Some island nations may be in a position to market certain services to other smaller and less developed nations. However, those smaller and less developed nations may be unable to generate such services themselves. The development potential of such service groups in SINs is clearly destination specific.

Feketekuty feels that a major problem for Third World countries in general is the need for skills, organization, and institutional environment, which are presupposed if world-class services are to be generated (1988, 120). Paralleling those needs is the problem of customer confidence. Many jurisdictions may have their markets constrained by foreign competition and customer interest, assuming that they produce the products in question. It would seem that facilitative services, although useful and even needed in the world economy, may have a modest developmental role in SINs. At least that seems to be so within the context of the discussion to date.

Perhaps the constraints alluded to above are most evident when specific SINs seek to market facilitating services to other Third World nations. In the Caribbean region there is some evidence that various jurisdictions have been successful in marketing specific services to customers in developed nations. The services in question were put forward by Demas and referred to earlier in the current discussion —

offshore university education, health, and financial and information processing. To those could be added tourism and the consumer services associated with it. Combinations of those service groups have become leading sectors of the economies of various Caribbean territories.

Tourism has had an impact throughout the Caribbean and Pacific regions, and issues relating to that industry are discussed in Chapter 5. By way of summary, the industry brings millions of visitors to the region. The impact varies from island to island because of accessibility and interest. The main gains are in the areas of employment and foreign exchange. The magnitude of those gains depends, in the case of employment, upon whether the industry generates genuine upwardly mobile career opportunities for the local population. In the case of foreign exchange, the cost of what must be imported must be weighed against generated net revenues. To complete the picture, the environmental and cultural costs of tourism must be assessed together with the impact of any overall adjustments in developmental priorities precipitated by the industry.

Within the context of services salable by small island economies to advanced nations, the observations of Harrison and Bluestone return to mind. In attempting to account for the growth of business services in advanced nations, they alluded to the emergence of a more complex technology and the spreading of production among widely separated locations. Certainly those factors have increased the need for a variety of sophisticated services in the international economy. Such services would include a wide range of specialized activities related to transportation and communications, not to mention engineering and construction. Whether any of those needs may work to the benefit of SINs would depend upon the role of the worldwide spread of production facilities. It would also depend upon whether such jurisdictions have a role in transportation and communications linkages in the international economy. The geographical positioning of the island nations in question would appear to be a major consideration. If they are positioned poorly with respect to the above considerations, various other business services, including finance, legal expertise, and accounting, cannot be considered as potential growth industries.

Despite what has just been suggested, one aspect of the new international economic environment appears to be benefitting certain small island locations. Once again the observations of Harrison and Bluestone hint at what has occurred. They are of the opinion that services expand "as businesses need to tend to their relations with more and more governments" (1988, 74). Often those relations have to do with the government regulation of corporate operating procedures. They may also concern matters relating to taxation or perhaps to the international transfer of financial assets. It has been suggested that "the emergence of Eurodollars to prominence as an international medium of exchange has led to a prolif-eration of financial centers geared towards the needs of the world market" (McKee, 1988, 126).

Many of these centers are housed in smaller economies. "Countries with very small, open economies have often embraced the financial secrecy business as a way of promoting economic development" (Walter, 1985, 93). According to Walter there are two kinds of financial centers active today: functional centers, "where transactions are actually under-taken and value added is created in the design and delivery of financial services," and booking centers, "where actions are recorded but the value-added involved is actually created elsewhere" (1985, 94). Among the former centers he lists London, Singapore, Bahrain, and Hong Kong; the latter includes the Bahamas, Cayman Islands, Seychelles, and Vanu-atu. Additional centers of this type have also come into existence, e.g., the Cook Islands in the Pacific. Among the potential benefits from becoming a financial center, Walter cites "indexed employment, fiscal contributions, and positive linkage effects to firms and industries that service the financial sector" (1985, 94).

Offshore banking and related activities in business and finance are emerging as a very popular option among the small economies of the Caribbean Basin region. That there is a market for such services in the world economy recalls the remark by Harrison and Bluestone concerning business having to contend with more and more governments.

It seems rather clear that among the services multinational enterprises purchase through offshore financial centers is distance from various gov-ernment rules and regulations. By manipulating their transactions in various nations through the books of banks and/or subsidiaries in offshore centers, they may be able to reduce tax payments and repatriate more profits. Captive insurance enables major corporations to insure themselves against certain risks, thus evading cumbersome insurance regulations and high commercial premiums. The parking of funds may enable banks to evade domestic onshore banking regulations in order to maximize speculative opportunities in foreign exchange markets. The positioning of actual banks or deposit desks in offshore locations may provide banks with a greater potential for deposits in the form of flight capital, estate moneys, and other funds attracted by the service of secrecy. Incorporation options provide additional opportunities to remove funds from the limelight in onshore jurisdictions. The flagging of shipping provides an opportunity to avoid stringent regulations involving operating procedures and employment practices, not to mention taxes once again.

Whether all these activities generate strong positive impacts upon economies hosting them remains to be seen. Certainly they will require many auxiliary business and accounting services, as well as legal and trust expertise. Such requirements should provide a number of professional and semiprofessional employment opportunities for local citizens. Whether attractive employment opportunities will emerge within the offshore service operations themselves will depend upon what arrangements are negotiated regarding the hiring and promotion of foreign personnel versus the training and absorption of domestic aspirants to the offshore financial labor force.

Some think that such activities will have little positive impact upon host jurisdictions. It has been suggested that large numbers of banks, insurance companies, and other financial corporations use the Caribbean to "seek vacations from an array of government regulations" (Barry et al., 1984, 125). Such firms "conduct hundreds of billions of dollars' worth of offshore transactions — meaning business that has little or no effect on the residents or the economy of the place of business" (Barry et al., 1984, 125). The accuracy of this appraisal is not clear. Such centers show wide variations in degrees of success. The Bahamas, for example, with a wide range of offshore activity certainly has gained a considerable number of employment opportunities through those activities. Still there is the suspicion that the Bahamian economy may not have experienced quite the benefits that planners had anticipated. The government at this writing (February 1989) has become quite vocal in criticizing the banks.

If the Bahamian authorities are not quite satisfied with the benefits from offshore banking, it is nonetheless clear that the Bahamas and the Cayman Islands, by their notable incursions into offshore banking circles, make it much more difficult for other Caribbean jurisdictions seeking to replicate their real or presumed success. The same may be said of Bermuda with respect to captive insurance. An unlimited number of centers in the same general region cannot succeed by competing in the same service. If offshore activities constitute a questionable development vehicle for jurisdictions that house them, their utility may be even more in doubt in the case of SINs aspiring to house them. Even if offshore financial services may have made very substantial contributions to the development of certain locations, that circumstance would hardly make the case for them as a general development vehicle.

Despite very real concerns with respect to the impact of services on the economies of SINs, there may be cases where they provide more scope for development than any available alternatives. Services induced in a Keynesian sense by income earned by potential consumers are hardly the activities that planners can rely upon as vehicles for development. Services that facilitate the location of manufacturing activity in specified island nations may make a positive contribution to development, provided that potential difficulties relating to development occasioned by the manufacturing facilities are solved. Finally services that facilitate operations in the international economy may determine the direction of certain small island economies, but they can hardly be relied upon as a general solution for the problems small island economies are experiencing. All in all, it may be that services may account for a percentage of the labor force in SINs comparable to what is the case in advanced nations. Despite that possibility, the verdict on services as a vehicle for the development of SINs seems to be unclear.

4

The Nature and Impact of the Public Service Sector

Although the public sectors of SINs are absolutely small compared to larger nations, they are often large relative to other nonprimary sectors in island microstates. This is especially so in those microstates heavily supported by foreign aid. In many island countries of the Pacific, the government is the major employer of cash income-earners. The basic communal nature of societies (tribal and village communities) in the Pacific possibly means that there is little opposition to expansion of the public sector, especially when it is financed to a large extent by foreign aid. Furthermore, the scope for expanding the commercial cash sector appears to be severely constrained by lack of profitable business and institutional impediments such as the communal ownership of land and of marine areas on a village basis.

The budget receipts of many island governments in the Pacific are heavily dependent on foreign aid. In the Caribbean region it is much less a factor. Foreign aid covers the capital expenditure of most Pacific island countries, and in many cases it makes a contribution to operating expenses. Such aid, it can be argued, is an indirect way for foreign governments to provide income support to islanders (Tisdell, 1990). This indirect support at least provides the illusion of adding to productivity and, therefore, may be morally more acceptable to aid donors than direct income supplements. The transfer appears as a reward for effort rather than a handout. The income distribution consequences of it, however, depend in the Pacific upon the extent to which family members can secure employment in the public sector.

Given sharing arrangements in extended families in the Pacific, employment that leads to a higher income for one family member will lead to income redistribution to all family members. Thus the income support received by a family is dependent on enough of its members securing appropriate well-paying employment, and in many SINs this means employment in the public sector. But the distribution of employment in the public sector may not be impartial. Social ties and patron-client relationships play a major role in the distribution of job opportunities in many small island states.

The small size of states may have a number of socioeconomic consequences for their public sectors. Many small economies tend to suffer considerable diseconomies because of lack of scale in the administration of their public service, and often they cannot supply the full range of services provided by the public sector in large states. Furthermore, there is not scope for as much specialization in the type of employment in the public sector as in large economies. A specialist is likely to be underemployed in a small economy whereas in a larger economy a number of specialists in the same area (or even a greater degree of specialization) may find adequate scope for employment in the public sector. In a very small country, such as Tuvalu (7,000 inhabitants), very few inhabitants may have tertiary education. For example, there may be no resident capable of understanding cost-benefit analysis or appropriate project evaluation, which may mean that the small country is at a disadvantage.

Connell (1988, 4) argues convincingly that small states do not necessarily have greater social and political coherence than large states and that there is little evidence that the quality of their public decisions is better because of their smallness. This contrasts with the common view since the era of Rousseau and Hume that public decisions are likely to be superior in small states. Furthermore, Connell (1988, 4) argues "administrative costs are proportionately higher in IMS [island microstates], especially those most fragmented, because of the necessity to maintain roughly the same diversity of government functions as in larger states, and tasks are not always easily amalgamated." Very often small island states have to rely on larger countries to provide specialists to assist with public administration, e.g., conduct censuses.

According to Connell (1988, 5), "social ties in IMS are so powerful and pervasive that anonymity, impersonal role relationships and impartiality are difficult to maintain, hence the public service can rarely be politically neutral and corruption is almost inescapable." Individual public servants can have great influence on ministers and often have direct access to them using informal channels of communication, and advice and discussions are often unrecorded. Arthur Lewis has said that in small states in which everybody depends on the government consisting of a single party for something, most are reluctant to offend it. "The civil servants live in fear; the police avoid unpleasantness; the trade unions are tied to the party; the newspapers depend on government advertisements;

and so on. In cases where they are also corrupt, and playing with public funds the situation becomes intolerable" (Lewis, 1965, 16). Politicians are thus relatively unconstrained in using their posts to their personal advantage.

In the Caribbean area the nature and positioning of the public sector within the economic frameworks of specific jurisdictions is different from what seems to be the case in the Pacific. Unlike that region, there are no remaining indigenous cultures of any size or consequence. Thus governmental institutions owe their origins to practices established by various European powers during the colonial era. With the exception of Haiti, the French-speaking jurisdictions are considered to be integral parts of France itself and hence do not operate as independent states. Excluding the British Virgin Islands, the Cayman Islands, the Turks and Caicos Islands, and Bermuda (which is not really in the Caribbean), all the former British territories in the region are independent of Britain today.

Despite their independence, all of Britain's former island possessions have adopted variations of the governmental system of Great Britain, save for Trinidad and Tobago, which has opted for a republican form of government. Within the Commonwealth Caribbean the structure of the judiciary and various government departments, not to mention various quasi-public agencies, is modeled to some extent after British practices.

Certainly the small nations that have emerged in the Commonwealth Caribbean rely more in a relative sense on government employment than do larger, more developed nations. That is in the nature of the trappings of government in small states. Excess resources may be expended upon the operation of government departments, but these are a part of the price very small jurisdictions pay for nationhood. Incidents of favors and corruption do occur as do occasional governmental adventures–witness Grenada. By and large, however, the small nations of the Commonwealth Caribbean have carried out their governmental functions rather well within the constraints of size.

In the Pacific islands, government budgetary receipts come mainly from taxes (principally from taxes on imports, except in the larger islands where tax on personal income and corporate income is more important) and from foreign aid. Taking the seven countries, Fiji, Kiribati, Papua New Guinea, Solomon Islands, Tonga, Vanuatu, and Western Samoa, import duties are the largest single source of tax revenue, except in Fiji and Papua New Guinea. Taxes on imports are attractive because of the ease of their collection, and because imports tend to fluctuate less in value than exports, they are a more stable source of budgetary revenue than export taxes. Import tax rates (tariffs) are not usually uniform. Higher tariffs apply in those cases where it is government policy to discourage the consumption of luxury goods or to protect domestic producers. Concessions on, or exemptions from, tariffs apply when materials are imported for use in export production and, in some cases, for capital equipment needed for business enterprises.

The governments of many developing countries rely heavily on export levies on agricultural products as a source of revenue. This is, however, a very unstable source of income. In the past, Pacific island countries relied heavily on this source, but their export levies are now modest except in the case of the Solomon Islands where they account for about 13% of tax revenue. Taxes on exports have been reduced or abolished in most Pacific island nations in order to encourage agricultural production and exports.

Although income tax accounts for about 50% of tax receipts in Fiji and Papua New Guinea, it is of much less importance as a source of tax revenue in smaller Pacific island countries. The source of most income tax is the wages and salaries of public employees. These taxes can be easily collected at source, and the government is the major source of cash income, which is more easily taxed than subsistence income. Tax receipts from private commercial businesses have usually been low. This is so because they make a relatively small contribution to GDP, tax avoidance may be easier than for wage and salary earners, and tax concessions are available to stimulate investment in manufacturing, hotels, and tourist activities. Even though public enterprises are treated in the same manner as private enterprises for taxation purposes, because they make little or no profit, they contribute very little to public revenue. Income tax has not been imposed in Vanuatu, which makes it a tax haven in common with certain Caribbean jurisdictions. Tonga has a poll tax, which is simple to collect in the subsistence sector.

Although most small island countries have a narrow tax base, there are considerable differences in the sources of their budgetary income. For example, in the case of Papua New Guinea's budget, income from mining is an important revenue item. In 1987, it accounted for over 7% of the total budget revenue of Papua New Guinea (excluding foreign aid). But because mining prices are volatile, revenue from this source can fluctuate considerably, and the temporary closure of the huge Bougainville copper mine because of terrorist action will considerably reduce the income receipts of the government from mining.

The sources of income for the central government of Kiribati are interesting. In 1986, excluding external grants, approximately one-third of its revenue was obtained from amounts drawn from its reserve fund, which has been invested abroad to earn income. This fund was built up from levies (taxes) on phosphate exports, which have now been exhausted. In addition fishing royalties are a sizable income component of the revenue of the central government of Kiribati. In 1986 they accounted for more than 23% of its revenue (excluding aid). In the Solomon Islands export levies, principally on logs, accounted for over 10% of the tax revenue of the central government in 1987. Budgetary revenues in many small island countries are heavily influenced by the fortunes of a small number of industries. It might also be noted that in the smallest countries, e.g., in Kiribati, philatelic sales are a significant component of government revenue.

External grants are a significant source of budget receipts for many island countries. For example as calculated from tables in Browne and Scott (1989), external grants (aid) accounted for the following percentages of the budget receipts in 1987 of the countries indicated: Fiji (18.71), Kiribati (40.38, 1986), Papua New Guinea (22.48), Solomon Islands (30.32), Tonga (19.78, 1987/88), Vanuatu (43.95), and Western Samoa (27.26). Thus the relative importance of aid as a contribution to the budget of the central governments in these countries varied from about 18% to over 40%, making it an extremely important component and one demanding considerable attention from island governments.

It can be seen that the budget receipts of many island governments depend on a narrow tax base, are derived from sources some of which are unstable or in the past have proven to be unsustainable (such as the tax revenue from phosphate mined on Ocean Island, Kiribati), and depend heavily on foreign aid, the amount of which is at the discretion of foreign aid donors. This makes long-term government planning difficult. Furthermore, because the budgets of island countries are mainly spent on wages and salaries of public sector employees, any significant cut in budget receipts can have an adverse impact on public sector employment, the major source of employment in the cash sector. In turn that can be expected to have serious political ramifications, especially because public sector employment is a means for widespread income support in the Pacific given the extended family sharing ethic.

In the Caribbean region the situation with respect to government revenue varies considerably between jurisdictions. In 1988 the Bahamas received no public revenues from income taxes while Trinidad and Tobago relied upon income taxes for nearly 55% of government revenues (Inter-American Development Bank, 1989, 478). In Jamaica the comparable figure was in the 37% range, and in the Dominican Republic 18.5%.

The same report showed property taxes to be relatively inconsequential among the nations referred to above. In the Bahamas indirect taxes accounted for more than 84% of government revenues in 1988. In the Dominican Republic the comparable figure was in the 61% range, and in Jamaica it stood at 48.4%. In Trinidad and Tobago indirect taxes were less significant, standing in the 25% range (Inter-American Development Bank, 1989, 479).

That portion of indirect tax revenue raised through levies on international trade accounted for more than 63% of government revenue in the Bahamas in 1988. The comparable figure for the Dominican Republic stood in the 40% range. In Haiti it was nearly 15% while in Trinidad and Tobago it stood at 7.4%. Thus tax policies appeared to show little consistency among the nations illustrated in the report.

Data derived from World Bank research provide for comparisons between a selection of former British Territories in the Caribbean. Figures for Antigua and Barbuda for 1983 show consumption taxes accounting for 22% of current government revenue, with import duties a close second at 20.1% (World Bank, 1985a, 11). Other tax sources included income (13%), hotel and guest taxes (6.8%), and property taxes 1.6%). According to the report, current revenue collections fell by over 5% in 1983 after four years of increase at average annual rates of 20%. The drop was attributed to "a decline in consumption taxes and import duties due to lower levels of merchandise imports" and the possibility of "the increasing effect of import duty exemptions granted under the Fiscal Initiatives and Hotel Incentives Acts" (1985a, 11).

The nation had a low ratio of tax revenues to GDP, 18% in 1982, as compared to other members of the Organization of Eastern Caribbean States (OECS). Among those jurisdictions the ratio stood at 25% for Dominica, 21% for Grenada, 26% in St. Lucia, and 23% in St. Vincent and the Grenadines (1985a, 11–12).

World Bank investigators felt that the nation was in need of "an effective tax policy and general improvement in the tax administration" (1985a, 12). Specific recommendations included the need for collection and assessment to be the preserve of the same agency and enhanced penalties for nonpayment. It was also felt that many duties and taxes should be consolidated in the interest of greater efficiency and that a simplified sales or value added tax should be considered. In addition it was suggested that more attention should be given to measuring the costs of import exemptions (1985a, 1–13.)

In the case of the Bahamas, "The Government's policy of no personal or corporate income taxes, does limit the overall flexibility of the tax system and reduces the government's fiscal flexibility" (World Bank, 1986, 12). World Bank investigators found that heavy reliance was placed upon indirect taxation, particularly taxes on international trade, which amounted to 59% of public revenue in 1984 (1986, 12). The ratio of tax revenue to GDP stood at 16.1% in 1984.

According to World Bank investigators, "The Bahamas' tax structure is inelastic with respect to both money income and to increases in real national income" (1968, 14). The heavy reliance upon import duties makes the tax structure strongly regressive. In addition "ad hoc measures that have been adopted over the past decade have both complicated administration and compliance and increased the possibilities and success of evasion" (1986, 14).

In Dominica with a population of 76,500 in 1983, income taxes accounted for roughly 26% of government revenues in the 1984–1985 year.[1] Grenada with a population in the 92,000 range in 1984 showed more than 25% of its public revenues accruing from income taxes. St. Vincent and the Grenadines (population 114,000 circa 1983) relied on income taxes for roughly 25% of total government revenues in 1983. In St. Lucia a comparable figure was 26.5% for the 1984–1985 year. In St. Christopher and Nevis the figure was 8.2% in 1984. The practice of avoiding the taxing of income, which is a matter of policy in the Bahamas, is hardly a general tax posture in the Caribbean.

Turning to the expenditure of island governments, at least in the Pacific, the smaller islands spend proportionally less of their government receipts on social services, especially pensions, and on defense than most developed countries. For example in 1986, Kiribati spent only 1.8% of its central government expenditure on pensions. In Tonga in 1987–1988 pensions and gratuities amounted to only 2.1% of central government expenditure. In Kiribati, expenditure on natural resources by the central government exceeded that on health in 1986. Neither Kiribati nor Tonga indicates any defense expenditure in their summaries of public expenditure, so one can presume that it is very minor. Larger countries such as Papua New Guinea and Fiji do have more significant levels of defense expenditure. Although this has not been so in the past in the Pacific, in certain small island states in the Caribbean the chief role of the army appears to have been to maintain dictatorial rulers in power — witness historical experience in Haiti and the Dominican Republic, not to mention Cuba, which is of course a special case.

The expenditure of the central government of SINs in the Pacific as a proportion of their GDPs indicates how important government expenditure can be in relation to these economies. On the whole, the smaller the economy, the greater is government expenditure as a percentage of GDP. In 1987 (1986 for Kiribati and 1987–1988 for Tonga) these percentages were as follows for the island countries indicated: Fiji (29.4), Kiribati (86.5), Papua New Guinea (30.9), Solomon Islands (47.2), Tonga (45.0), Vanuatu (56.9), and Western Samoa (approximately 50.0). The 1986 figure for Kiribati is very high, but, since phosphate mining has ceased, this percentage has declined. Compared to most large nations these percentages are extremely large and highlight the dominating influence of the public sector on these island economies.

Some writers, such as Bertram (1986), are critical that the public sectors of these economies have been allowed to grow so large relative to the rest of the economy, partially because of support from foreign aid. They see such a development as "crowding out" traditional economic activities and increasing the exposure of small island economies to risk and foreign influence. What is clear is that a sector unable to sustain itself economically has been expanded to a dominant position and that this expansion is at the expense of economic self-reliance. In the Caribbean where foreign aid is less a factor the problem referred to above is not widespread.

Island countries in the Pacific have not been averse to establishing public enterprises. Browne and Scott (1989, 22) comment, "Overall, public enterprises have added to budgetary pressures rather than contributed to resource mobilization." They go on to suggest, "While some enterprises have earned considerable profits over a long period, including the corporations engaged in sugar production and distribution in Fiji and plantations in Solomon Islands, no country has been immune from these pressures." They add, "In the industrial and commercial fields, high wage costs, overstaffing and management problems have been common."

The islands have made their largest losses on their national airlines, many of which were set up partially for prestige purposes. For example, Nauru suffered heavy losses on its airline. Also there have been large losses on interisland shipping services. Problems have also emerged in energy supplies and public housing in urban areas because of low pricing policies.

In the 1980s many of the larger nations tried to privatize their public enterprises, but this trend was not apparent in the Pacific islands. However, several countries tried to restrict the formation of new public enterprises and subject existing ones to greater scrutiny in order to reduce losses.

Although banking is conducted mostly by private banks in the island countries of the Pacific, most have a central bank, and many have (public enterprise) development banks. These banks provide longer-term finance for private sector investment, mainly in agriculture and industry.

Although governments usually provide the equity capital for such banks, most of their loanable funds are supplied by multilateral financial institutions such as the World Bank and the Asian Development Bank, by bilateral donors, and by the European Economic Community. These loanable funds are generally provided on concessional terms by international suppliers and usually lent at rates of interest below the market rate. Browne and Scott (1989, 28) consider that the quality of loan portfolios held by the island development banks has been adversely affected by their staff's lack of experience in processing applications and by charging interest rates below market values. They suggest that "this has increased the likelihood of the allocation of funds to unprofitable activities and has contributed to the growth of loan arrears." Nevertheless, the availability of credit to small business has been improved by the creation of development banks, and in particular small urban business seems to have gained. Both the location of development banks and the nature of their loans have encouraged urbanization to some small extent.

Overall a major impact of the public sector in SINs has been to foster urbanization and centralization of economic activity. This has happened for several reasons. First, government offices and operations are located predominantly in urban areas, particularly capital cities. Second, subtracting leakages to overseas countries, secondary expenditure arising from original government expenditure in the capital city and urban areas has a strong tendency to be spent on goods and services from those areas and nearby. This provides a secondary demand — pull toward increased centralization and urbanization, which is reinforced by supply-side facilitators such as economies of agglomeration. Also the fact that some urban services are like localized quasi-public goods or localized pure public goods can also encourage urbanization and centralization (Tisdell, 1975). For example, the benefit from public goods available to each consumer location in an urban area may increase as the scale of provision of a quasi-public good increases up to a point. Hence, as an urban area expands and its available pure public goods expand, it can become more attractive to immigrants, who by locating in the area can enjoy its public goods aspects. As mentioned earlier, the public sector may also have a crowding out effect on agriculture, especially if the inflow of foreign aid leads to an appreciation of the currency, making it more difficult for agriculture to export. In the latter case the so-called Dutch disease is also present (cf., Bertram, 1986).

In archipelagic nations there has been a strong trend toward greater urbanization and toward greater centralization on the island containing the nation's capital city. Because of internal migration, outer islands are becoming depopulated. To a considerable extent the growth of the government sector has facilitated and fostered this pattern of development.

Turning to another distorting influence of the public sector, the prospect of employment in the public sector in many island nations, particularly in the Pacific, has exerted a disproportionate influence on the education system. The skills and knowledge imparted to students are usually those of greatest value for entry to the public service rather than for commerce, trades, or agriculture. Educated individuals tend to migrate toward urban areas hoping to gain employment, and as a rule the superior educational institutions are also located in larger urban areas. Given the type of education received, many would prefer to remain unemployed or underemployed in an urban area rather than choose manual work in the countryside.

In conclusion, the public sector of many SINs clearly suffers from *absolute* smallness compared to larger nations. A full range of public services of the type supplied in larger nations probably cannot be efficiently provided; distance and impersonal role-playing is difficult to maintain in the public sector; and corruption, patron-client relationships, and meddling in public service affairs may thrive in some cases. The tax base of island governments is frequently narrow, sometimes difficult to sustain, and, at least in the Pacific, there is a high degree of dependence on foreign aid as a contribution to budget receipts. The small nations in question must devote considerable effort to cultivating this source and to ensuring that this support is sustained, for it can be subject to unanticipated variation. Also, the possibility of public sector employment shapes education programs in some cases, and the growth of this sector is possibly the major factor contributing to increasing urbanization and centralization in many island states.

NOTE

1. Assessments of the importance of income taxes in the OECS members discussed here were derived from World Bank reports prepared for Dominica, Grenada, St. Christopher and Nevis, St. Lucia, and St. Vincent and the Grenadines. The pertinent reports are all contained in the bibliography and are not referred to by name in the text.

5

The Structural and Employment Impacts of Tourism

In recent years advances in the technology of transportation and communications have led to the democratization of international tourism. Today attractively priced vacation packages are available to large numbers of potential customers who previously would have found such leisure-time options well beyond their means. Those employed in the marketing of international vacation packages have been quick to broaden the menu of destinations offered. As competition intensifies in the travel industry, the trend toward more vacation destinations and wider ranges of leisure-time activities probably will continue as travel professionals attempt to maintain or augment their profit shares.

In this climate, it is hardly surprising that Third World nations have become attractive to tourism professionals. Low labor costs, coupled with the potential for marketing attractive settings for leisure-time activities, not to mention "authentic cultural experiences," have stimulated this advance on the part of potential host countries. The prospect of earning foreign exchange credit, coupled with presumed employment opportunities in tourist facilities and related service pursuits, is proving to be seductive.

In the face of such momentums, many Third World countries have become hosts to international tourism with seemingly little planning or forethought with respect to the actual demands or impacts that the industry may make upon their economies, much less upon reasonable developmental objectives. The potential for difficulties seems to be inversely related to the size and economic strength of the nations concerned. Basically the smaller Third World nations are among those

An earlier version of this chapter appeared as "Tourism as an Industry for the Economic Expansion of Archipelagoes and Small Island States," in *Massey Journal of Asian and Pacific Business,* Volume 3, Number 1, 1988. Used with permission.

where the ascendancy of tourism seems most enticing. The present discussion concerns itself with a set of actual or potential difficulties associated with the rise of tourism in SINs. In the course of the discussion, the authors draw upon personal observations involving tourism in the Caribbean, the South Pacific, and elsewhere. By so doing, it is hoped that a better basis for policy formulation can be suggested whereby small nations contemplating tourist development may be able to realize actual gains from the industry while minimizing certain negative externalities.

As summarized by Dwyer (1986, 1–2), national development plans for South Pacific countries see the tourist industry as contributing to many goals. These "include goals such as increasing foreign exchange earnings, to reduce balance of payments deficits, the generation of employment, the establishment of positive and mutually supportive linkages with other sectors of the economy, reducing the reliance on imports, while at the same time preserving traditional values and cultures."

Similar views of tourism and the development process have been put forward concerning the Caribbean. "If there is one single industry that has been heralded as a pathway from economic servitude to certain progress, it is tourism" (Cross, 1979, 11). Cross cites the industry as the "greatest generator of foreign exchange" in some cases and as the major employer in the Netherlands Antilles and the Bahamas with a "major role in a number of Leeward and Windward Islands." Tourist expenditures in the Caribbean have been seen to provide various nations "with a major portion of their foreign exchange earnings" (Hope, 1986b, 90). This aspect was thought to be the most noticeable benefit from the industry.

It seems appropriate to weigh the realism of these and similar expectations. Both Cross and Hope appeared to have reservations concerning the overall impact of tourism. Small states in the Caribbean (e.g., the Bahamas, Jamaica), in the Pacific (e.g., Cook Islands, Tonga, Fiji), and in the Indian Ocean (e.g., the Maldives and the Seychelles) are eagerly encouraging foreign tourism as a means for economic growth. In so doing, they wish to share in the expansion of an industry that is growing worldwide and expect this industry to provide a growth pole (Perroux, 1950; 1970; McKee, 1987). However, how effective is the tourist industry likely to be as a means for economic development? It is not, as shown below, a panacea for obtaining regional decentralization nor for limiting urbanization. It has limitations as a means for increasing domestic income and employment. It can have adverse income distributional consequences and create balance of payment problems. Especially in small states, it can be a risky or unstable source of foreign income and can undermine traditional industries. It can have adverse and irreversible social and environmental consequences, which may be particularly evident in small states.

A number of small South Pacific nations have considerably expanded the economic significance of their tourist industries in the last decade and have become heavily dependent on it. These nations include Tonga, Fiji, Vanuatu, and Western Samoa. In 1984 gross tourist receipts as a percentage of all exports amounted to about 68% for Tonga, 35% for Fiji, 27% for Vanuatu, and 25% for Western Samoa and, as a percentage of GDP, to 13.5%, 22%, 10.5%, and 4% respectively (Dwyer, 1986, 16). Tourism is by far Tonga's most important export industry, Fiji's major source of foreign earnings, and Vanuatu's second most important earner of foreign exchange.

Tourism is making similar inroads upon economies in the Caribbean region. "Tourism is the most important sector of the Bahamian economy, accounting for about one-third of GDP and employing, directly and indirectly, over half of the working population" (World Bank, 1986, 22). The industry was also identified as the single most important economic activity in Antigua and Barbuda (World Bank, 1985a). Various World Bank reports have alluded to the potential of the industry in smaller Caribbean locations. The economic health and impact of this industry seem to be of great concern in both the South Pacific and the Caribbean. This chapter considers the possible consequences of the development of tourism for regional decentralization and urbanization, income distribution, employment, and balance of payments.

It is tempting to believe that a tourist industry based on natural attractions will be a force in the decentralization of population. In archipelagoes, for example, it may be tempting to suggest that it will cause movement of population toward outer islands and away from capital cities and islands containing these. Many tourists ostensibly visit SINs because of their natural attractions and the desire to escape from urbanization. But does tourism really promote decentralization?

Before turning to this question, it should be noted that many archipelagic states are concerned about the depopulation of their outer islands and internal migration, which is causing increased urbanization and the rapid growth of their capital cities. Problems are being experienced in supplying adequate infrastructure for capital cities and their environs. Urban unemployment (sometimes accompanied by high crime rates) is rising, and natural environments are being overtaxed. This movement to central places is combined with a decline in traditional primary industries, which leads to higher imports of primary products.

In addition, there is a decline in subsistence agriculture so that these economies become more dependent on trade and imports for their economic welfare. Tourism and the external linkages that it requires complicate this situation. The tastes of the visitors generate a need for food imports, which in turn may create a demonstration effect among certain elements of the local population. Once again the result is an increase in food imports, which may have an undesirable impact on trade balances and which may even affect domestic food production. This may be a special problem in archipelagic SINs where the demonstration effect, combined with economies of scale with respect to food imports, may make it very difficult for domestic food producers to compete in supplying the needs of the urbanized population. Farmers and fishermen in more remote areas may find their local markets depleted through the migration of populations to urban areas and that they are unable to access the markets of those growing areas. In the pecking order established by tourism and its external linkages, traditional food suppliers can expect little government aid with respect to an infrastructure that would provide them with access to domestic markets.

The concern for the decline in subsistence agriculture and subsequent increases in import dependencies is widespread. In this respect see, for example, Fisk (1985) in relation to Kiribati, Fairbairn (1985, Ch. 13) in relation to the Cook Islands, and Bertram and Watters (1985) in relation to SINs in the South Pacific generally.

The phenomenon is not confined to the South Pacific. With respect to the Caribbean, the need for an integrated rural development has been recognized (Hope, 1986b, 76) as has the need for import substitution with respect to food supplies. In the Bahamas the government restricts granting import licenses during periods when local food supplies are available (World Bank, 1986, 31).

Tourism is essentially a service industry. As McKee (1987, 173) has noted, service industries tend to be urban orientated. This raises the question of whether tourism is likely to be different in its orientation to other service industries.

In our view, tourism does have an orientation toward central places in SINs, even though the strength of the orientation is weaker than for other service industries such as banking and retailing. The urban orientation of tourism comes about in SINs because of the location of tourist facilities and resorts in and near larger urban centers, usually capital cities, and because of the backward linkages of tourism to inputs supplied principally by or through larger urban centers.

Certainly mass marketed tourism conforms to that configuration. Major tourist concentrations tend to cluster in and around urban centers. However, highly specialized top of the line facilities may seek out less crowded domains. In the Caribbean area the Bahamas may be a case in point. The most obvious tourist destinations are the islands of New Providence (Nassau) and Grand Bahamas (Freeport). Both of those destinations boast the ability to accommodate thousands of visitors and feature an extensive menu of leisure-time activities. Together they account for the bulk of tourist traffic in the Bahamas. However, some of the less accessible islands harbor resorts frequented by the world's elite. Although air service does exist between New Providence and these secondary destinations, the bulk of the population of the more remote islands still relies on mail boats as the principle contact with Nassau. There is little evidence that the jet set facilities located on the more remote islands have done much to integrate the archipelago. Indeed one of the elements attracting wealthy vacationers may well be isolation. Examples of similar character can be found in the archipelago housing the U.S. and British Virgin Islands.

A number of factors probably contribute to this orientation. First, points of entry (gateways) to a country such as airports and harbors tend to be in capital cities or nearby, and the majority of tourists come in through such gateways. Entry and departure formalities are frequently centralized at such points, and the international transport industry draws on services and inputs that usually can be provided only in or near a large urban center. The further a tourist moves beyond his or her point of entry to a country, the greater is the cost and the time required. This is especially so in archipelagic states because communication links with more distant islands are often infrequent, and commonly the journey has to be by boat because air links are not available. This is likely to deter the majority of foreign tourists, who are on a limited financial budget and a limited time budget, from traveling a long distance from their point of entry.

In addition, foreign tourists often demand facilities that are available only within proximity to urban centers, such as a range of shopping choices, access to medical and related facilities in case of accident or ill health, adequate communication with the rest of the world, and a variety of attractions including organized cultural activities. Imported goods that tourists rely on to a considerable extent are likely to be more costly and less available in areas remote from ports where they enter the country.

Furthermore, from the point of view of operators or owners of tourist facilities, several factors favor concentration close to urban centers and gateways. Their backward linkages are to such areas. For example, the connections of tourist resorts with tourist agents are likely to be facilitated the closer their proximity. The services tourist resorts require to support tourist operations are more readily available and less costly to obtain when they are located near major urban centers. In addition, a larger pool of manpower is available to tourist resorts in the vicinity of a large urban area. Also less fluctuation in capacity utilization of tourist facilities is likely to occur (because of the operation of the probability law of large numbers) in an area where a larger pool of tourists is allocated among a greater number of resorts or hotels, as is normally the case in a central-ized or relatively centralized place.

Many of the owners and overall supervisors of tourist resorts live in major urban areas in SINs. Head offices may be located in capital cities or in overseas countries. To the extent that absentee owners or overall managers are either located in large urban areas or would arrive at such centers when traveling from overseas, they may prefer tourist centers not to be too distant from these urban areas. Otherwise, monitoring and overall direction of tourist centers becomes difficult because of the time and cost involved in visiting remote localities.

The above factors suggest that tourism in SINs is likely to have an urban or central area location bias, directly and indirectly, because of the urban-specific nature of many of the inputs required by the industry. Considerable empirical evidence supports the view that tourist areas tend to be concentrated at/or near a central place or island area in archipelagic SINs. Take the case of the Maldives. Of the 54 holiday resorts that had been established in the Maldives by 1984, 43 were located in Male atoll, which contains the capital city, and of the remainder, most were located in nearby Alifu atoll. In terms of tourist bed-capacity the concentration is even more marked: 3,934 of the available 4,676 beds, or 84%, were located in Male atoll according to "Statistics of the Department of Tourism, Male." If the beds in Alifu atoll are also included, 95% of tourist beds are located in or near Male atoll. Very few tourist beds are located in the more remote atolls.

Frequently growth of the tourist industry in developing countries is encouraged in the belief that it is a labor-intensive industry and, there-fore, involves a composition of factors of production appropriate to relative factor availability in those countries. However, evidence indi-cates that tourism is a capital-intensive industry on the whole, especially if its social infrastructure requirements are taken into account. Trans-port tends to be capital-intensive as does telecommunication, and this is also the case for hotels and related facilities. The low labor-intensity of the industry seems to be borne out by Varley (1978), who found that the employment generating effect of tourism in Fiji was less than for most industries.

In addition, much of the employment involved in tourism requires skills that are in short supply in developing countries, especially SINs. Frequently, managers, accountants, head chefs, and, in some cases, second-level management personnel are brought from more developed countries. In many cases, too, it is necessary for tourist personnel to have at least some knowledge of foreign languages and foreign customs. In consequence, employment of locals may not be preferred, and few positions may become available for the uneducated.

There are many examples of this. Mishra (1982), for example, observed that the creation of Chitwan National Park in Nepal, while attracting foreign tourists, has not generated jobs for locals despite the tourist industry's promise. Because of lack of local education, few locals are employed, and those employed have menial jobs. Most of the well-paying jobs are obtained by qualified and experienced people outside Nepal. Much the same position has been observed in the Maldives (Sathiendrakumar and Tisdell, 1985).

There is also concern on another score. The employment-generating effects of tourism seem to be low in SINs. As mentioned above, Varley (1978) estimated, using multiplier analysis, that the employment-generating impact of tourism in Fiji was less than all primary and secondary industry and less than the average of other tertiary sectors. As Dwyer (1986, 21) observes, tourism compared to other sectors of the economy does not create a significant demand for labor in Fiji.

Dwyer (1986, 22) emphasizes the importance of taking into account the opportunity costs of expanding employment in the tertiary sector, especially where manpower is diverted from the primary and secondary sectors of the economy, and Ganilau (1974, 67–68) has expressed particular concern about such diversion from agriculture. "This may well conflict with rural development objectives especially if the individuals who divert are the more enterprising and able members of the rural population. While there is some evidence that the cost of providing each tourism job tends to be very high compared to agriculture" (UNDP, 1984), there has been no detailed study of this for the South Pacific (Dwyer, 1986, 22).

In many instances, employment in the tourist industry is seasonal. Although this can be a disadvantage, it is not necessarily so for temporary migrants in developing countries who can return home during the tourist off-season and help in their villages.

Growth of the tourist industry can increase inequality of income in SINs. The better educated and skilled are likely to be advantaged whereas the unskilled and less educated are likely to be disadvantaged. Evidence from the Maldives indicates that it is mostly the more educated and economically more affluent who have benefitted most from opportunities for employment in the growing tourist industry (see Sathiendrakumar and Tisdell, 1987).

Also, tourist development may lead to exclusion of locals from areas set aside for foreign tourists. Common access or common land may be appropriated for international tourist use. This means that the local poor may no longer have access to such land for enjoyment and for food gathering. So the local poor may be deprived of a part of their means of subsistence.

In addition, demand by tourists for consumption of local products such as fish, prawn (shrimp), or fruits may disadvantage poorer domestic consumers in the society. They may find their real income reduced because the demands of foreign tourists force up the price of these goods. Domestic consumers may be forced to forgo consumption of these now higher priced local goods and substitute consumption of lower quality local goods. In Thailand, some locals complain that they can no longer afford to purchase cashews and prawns produced in their own country. Jeffries (1982) has pointed out that tourism in the Mt. Everest area has led to increased food and fuel prices and an increasing dependence of locals on imported goods. Imports of kerosene and of tinned foods for local consumption have increased.

However, local consumers are not always disadvantaged in this way, and in some fortunate cases foreign tourists demand local products for which there is no local demand. For instance, in the Maldives local people eat tuna, not reef fish. Tourists, however, have a demand for reef fish. Thus tourists have created a demand for a resource previously unutilized.

The impact of tourism on the balance of payments of a country can be deceptive. Tourism can add substantially to gross receipts, but its contributions to net receipts may be small if a considerable amount of the commodities required by tourists have to be imported.

Import leakages from foreign tourist expenditures in small island economies may be substantial. Speaking of Western Samoa, Dwyer (1986, 17, 18) had observed leakages for hotel and other food consumption between 65% and 75% and for beverages 50%. Among other tourist related items with high import contents were "hotel costs — construction materials 75–85%, equipment in excess of 90%, operational requirements

50–60%, electric power costs 50%" (Dwyer, 1986, 17, 18). According to Dwyer, some items related to transportation, including fuel, were 100% imported. In an attempt to make his observations more general, he suggested, "Even in the case of Fiji, with its more diverse manufacturing base, the most recent estimate is that leakages constitute 75% of gross tourist expenditure" (Fiji, 1983, 25).

In addition, contact of foreign tourists with host country residents is likely to have a demonstration effect. As mentioned earlier the food habits of local residents may alter, and this may necessitate greater imports. Changes in food habits are not always nutritionally advantageous, and other adopted consumption patterns, such as increased alcohol consumption, may be damaging to the health of individuals and the normal functioning of families and sociological groups.

Where tourist facilities are operated by multinational companies, there may be a high propensity to import. Such companies often try to standardize their service equipment internationally and source supply from international sources (United Nations, 1982). Furthermore, even when the tourist industry does buy local products, these are frequently supplied by local subsidiaries of foreign firms that typically import a high proportion of their raw materials (Dwyer, 1986, 17).

Import dependence of the tourist industry in SINs is likely to be greater than in large developing countries. They are likely to produce a greater range of commodities locally than SINs, and so a greater proportion of foreign tourist demands can be met from local sources. McKee (1985, 171) has observed that tourist-related import substitution as a propellant for local economic activity declines in feasibility directly with the size and viability of the host economy.

Tourism is a worldwide growth industry, but it is a risky industry because the sale of its product to foreigners requires them to visit the country. Demand for visits can decline precipitously if political or social disturbances occur in the host country or if air piracy becomes common in the area or if public safety is threatened. From this point of view, it appears to be much riskier than traditional export industries. This is illustrated by recent events in Fiji, where the elected government was ousted and a number of incidents involving foreign tourists have been reported.

A further difficulty is that the assets used by the tourist industry tend to be relatively specific to that industry. A decline in demand for tourist facilities results in large sunk costs. In contrast, this is not usual for most agricultural industries because capital such as tractors can be switched from growing one type of crop to another if the export demand for a particular crop declines.

If a SIN does achieve a substantial net balance of payments surplus from tourism, it faces an additional difficulty. Its exchange rate may appreciate and cause a decline in traditional export industries such as agriculture. Thus it encourages de-agriculturalization, and, as a consequence, its exports are less diversified and the economy may exhibit symptoms of the "Dutch Disease" (Gillis et al., 1983).

SINs need to realize that development of a tourist industry is not a magical means of overcoming their economic difficulties. It can be a disappointing means of promoting decentralization of population and industry and of stemming the depopulation of outer islands and may prove to be an inadequate means of raising host country incomes and employment. It can worsen income distribution, reduce welfare, and have adverse consequences for the balance of payments, traditional industries, and the environment. It is a volatile and risky export industry subject to disturbance from a wide range of factors, including political instability, and it may be difficult to sustain should environmental deterioration occur, for instance, as a result of pressures caused by tourism itself. Added to these problems is the fair weather nature of the industry, its susceptibility to being influenced by external forces beyond its control, which can clog up its profit potential and idle its facilities (McKee, 1988, 96).

This is not to claim that the tourist industry has no role in the development of SINs. Rather it is a warning against heavy reliance on this industry for economic development. Governments need to monitor its impact and place limitations on its growth where appropriate. The unfettered development of this industry is unlikely to be in the national interest.

II

Demographic and Socioeconomic Issues

6

Urbanization and the Development Problem

In recent years, a veritable deluge of work has appeared, all of which has purported to contribute to the understanding of the continuing migration of rural populations toward the major metropolitan areas of Third World nations. Some of this literature concerns itself with the causes and effects of such migrations while another stream of investigations has moved in the direction of urban growth and problems related to labor absorption.

So intense has been the interest in the burgeoning urban complexes of the Third World that economists and other professionals who have become involved have often been accused of having an urban bias. The current authors, while not accepting such a label, are nonetheless concerned with the phenomenon of urban expansion in Third World settings and the effects that such expansion appears to be having upon development processes and the setting of national priorities to facilitate those processes.

Much of the available literature pertains to the problems precipitated by the emergence of very large metropolitan complexes in Third World settings. The current authors are concerned with problems related to urban impact on ministates, more specifically, SINs. These newly emergent states may be experiencing problems related to urbanization, similar in nature, if not in extent, to those that have been documented in larger emerging nations. It is hoped the current discussion places some of these problems in perspective. More specifically it will address the impact that urbanization appears to be having upon the developmental prospects of SINs. In so doing it will rely upon practical examples from the Caribbean region, the South Pacific, and other areas.

An earlier version of this chapter appeared in *METU Studies in Development,* Volume 16, Numbers 1–2, 1989. Used with permission.

On the surface it would appear that SINs should not be experiencing the urban problems highlighted in the literature on Third World urbanization because many of those problems appear to emanate from diseconomies of scale generated by overurbanization. This supposition is an oversimplification. In the Caribbean region alone Havana, San Juan, and Santo Domingo would have to be considered as major metropolitan areas by any reasonable standard. Granted that Havana and San Juan are housed in political jurisdictions that may not be germane to the present discussions, their existence together with that of Santo Domingo suggests that SINs are not immune to the emergence of rather large conurbations.

It is tautological to suggest that the only real limit to urban expansion is the population of the nation in question and its propensity to increase. That being the case, it is theoretically possible for some SINs to become little more than city-states as have Hong Kong and Singapore. The macroeffects that urbanization may have upon national development patterns, rather than its intraurban microeffects, i.e., urban problems per se, constitute the major concern of the current authors. A reasonable taxonomy of the latter based upon evidence from the Caribbean is already available (Hope, 1986b).

In SINS the shift of the economy from a focus on agriculture to a manufacturing/service base may cause even more impetus to population movements than has been the case in larger Third World nations. The neoclassical explanation for such population movements revolved around expectations of surplus rural labor of attaining employment in urban areas. In the initial version of the model (Lewis, 1954), rural to urban migration would continue as long as it was feasible for new urban arrivals to attain employment at an urban subsistence wage (cf., Tisdell and Fairbairn, 1984). The pressure of the influx would presumably ensure that wages would stay at that level and that the capitalists by reinvesting their gains would cause the economy to grow, thus permitting the absorption of new in-migrants on a continuing basis until subsistence wages were being earned in both rural and urban sectors of the economy.

Without reviewing the increasing eloquence of that line of reasoning over the period since its inception, suffice it to say that there appear to be frictions associated with the orderly and predictable absorption of in-migrants into the modern sectors of the urban labor force in major Third World metropolitan areas — witness the continuing expansion of what has come to be called the urban informal sector and what may be forms of disguised urban unemployment and all the difficulties that those phenomena appear to have bred. It even seems as though the equilibrating logic may be better applied to the informal sector itself because the urban influx is continuing without much evidence that entry to the modern sector is readily available (McKee, 1988). Thus it would appear that this neoclassical hybrid does supply some degree of understanding concerning the continuing rural-to-urban migration that various Third World nations are experiencing, especially when linked to the Todaro, rural-urban migration model, which regards "expected" real wage gains (in the probabilistic sense) as an important determinant of migration decisions (Todaro, 1989; 1969).

Whether or not the same logic can be used effectively to explain urban development in SINs remains to be seen. What has been occurring in those jurisdictions can hardly be considered a microcosm of the experience of larger nations. Nonprimary elements of the modern sectors of SINs are generally housed in urban areas, but they may be substantially different in structure from their counterparts in metropolitan complexes in large Third World nations.

Many island ministates were formerly colonies or possessions of various developed nations. This is certainly true of most of the SINs in the Caribbean and the South Pacific. In many such states the principal urban agglomeration served various governmental and administrative functions during the period of foreign domination. Various commercial functions housed in such urban centers today date from the colonial era as well. In many cases these centers also served various functions relating to transportation and communications in as much as linkages were required with the external world. Such linkages during the colonial period were doubtless embryonic by current standards. Nonetheless, they required an infrastructure that has been improved in ways that have permitted such centers to maintain their external linkage functions.

In many cases they have developed deepwater port facilities. Often airports have been constructed to service them. In the Caribbean, cruise ships may have replaced produce carriers at the docks. Hotels have been constructed to accommodate tourist and convention traffic as well as day-to-day business travelers. Some ministates have encouraged the development of international banking facilities with varying degrees of success. In short the urban centers in many SINs have become the seat of a rather sophisticated array of services geared to the international economy and perhaps only peripherally to the domestic needs of the nations in question. The infrastructure requirements of these urban service economies are often given priority over domestic needs in governmental pecking orders. Thus a certain continuity is maintained with the Colonial era when infrastructures were designed to facilitate the export of staples rather than to encourage domestic economic integration (McKee, 1977).

To the extent that urban centers in small island states have assumed much of the economic configuration outlined above, their impact with respect to the national economy may be very different proportionally from that of major urban centers in larger Third World nations. Despite the major influence that the latter centers are having for good or ill on developmental prospects in certain nations, the effects of urban centers on the ministates that house them may be far greater in a comparative sense. Circumstances may have underwritten that often discussed urban policy bias to such an extent that priorities have been adjusted to what have been referred to above as city-states.

Postponing any utilitarian judgments concerning such circumstances, it might be well to review the expository strength of the neoclassical model of urban expansion as it pertains to SINs. To some extent the model may differ in its application according to geographical constraints present in individual SINs. For example, the Bahamas and Barbados, two independent nations, were almost equal in population in 1986 (Inter-American Development Bank, 1987).[1] However the Bahamas consist of an archipelago of some 700 islands, total land area 4,404 square miles, with some 20 inhabited. Barbados is a single island with a total land area of 161 square miles.

Barbados, with its history of plantations, had an agricultural sector that accounted for only 8.4% of the island's workforce in 1983 although nearly 68% of the total population was classed as rural residents. Some of the nonagricultural rural residents may have been employed in tourist resorts along the west and south coasts of the island in strips of development radiating outward from Bridgetown, the nation's capital. If the data presented above are accurate, Bridgetown has a population of less than 100 thousand. The figure given may understate the actual size of the city by drawing boundaries along parish lines rather than considering the contiguous urban area.

Despite the explanatory limitations of the data, Bridgetown is clearly an urban complex of the sort alluded to earlier, in which a rather extensive service sector dominates the urban economy. In addition to a public service component dating from colonial times, the metropolitan area boasts a commercial and retail complex that caters to international as well as domestic tastes. The financial sector, notably banking, offshore insurance, and ship registration, has received recognition as a secondary offshore investment center, and the government is encouraging the nurture of such activities. Tourism is a large and growing industry. Eliminating manufacturing, construction, and agriculture from the workforce leaves a residual of 67%, which is undoubtedly composed of public and private service pursuits with very large urban components. Clearly the city and the transportation and communications infrastructure that has been been built up around it asserts an influence in the national economy proportionally much more significant than what might be expected from much larger urban complexes in mainland nations.

What has been said of Bridgetown is even truer of Nassau with respect to the Bahamas. In the Bahamas nearly 84% of the labor force is employed in pursuits other than the primary sector, construction, and manufacturing, and more than 54% of the population was considered to be urban in 1986. New Providence, the island housing Nassau, accounts for more than half the nation's population. The expansion of metropolitan Nassau has absorbed what were once small independent urban clusters.

Nassau is the nation's capital and administrative center. It is the site of a major deepwater port, through which much of the nation's imports are funneled. The port is also one of the busiest cruise ship destinations in the entire Caribbean region, and the city and its environs have become a world-class tourist destination. Nassau is also a major offshore banking center with state-of-the-art communications linkages to the world's major financial centers. The city's commercial district has become a shopping center for luxury goods.

Although small aircraft ply back and forth between Florida and airstrips on islands in the Bahamas and the major airport at Freeport on Grand Bahama, Nassau and/or the island of New Providence is definitely the major transportation hub for the entire archipelago. From Nassau Harbour mail boats service the less populated islands, carrying passengers and freight. *Bahamas Air*, the nation's flagship carrier, also services certain smaller island airstrips on a regular basis. Thus the other islands have reasonable access to Nassau. However, commercial and/or government-sponsored transportation linkages between islands other than New Providence are spotty at best. The other islands are on the spokes of a wheel that has no real unifying rim. Even Freeport/Lucaya, the nation's second city, has few commercial transportation linkages with domestic other-island destinations beyond New Providence. Thus there is little inter-island movement of people and materials, and the owners of foreign pleasure craft are more apt to become familiar with a variety of island destinations than are the domestic population.

From this brief discussion it can be seen that the Bahamas and Barbados, despite similarities in population size, are very different economically. Barbados has made a transition from the primacy of plantation agriculture to an urban-oriented service economy. Because the island is so small, this transition has been made without any obvious influx of surplus labor to the capital. This is not to say that the nation is without economic concerns. Under a continuing threat from overpopulation, it could undoubtedly benefit from import substitution in the area of food production. The need to import the bulk of goods it requires is a problem common to many SINs. In a very real sense, it must rely upon its external service component to underwrite its hopes of further material enhancement. The labor absorption problem revolves around the skills required in the well-paying service pursuits. Many such positions in finance, tourism, and transportation and communications may not be open to substantial portions of the labor force and, in fact, may be staffed by foreign nationals on a continuing basis. Obviously, economic growth requires progress on that particular issue. Assuming that the upward mobility of labor can be encouraged, it is conceivable that Barbados and certain similarly appointed SINs can make economic progress through reliance upon an externally oriented service sector. However entry to the pecking order of viable international service centers is constrained by world demand, not to mention existing centers, whether housed in SINs or elsewhere. Thus development plans based on such service scenarios may fall short of expectations in some SINs simply because similar plans have succeeded elsewhere.

Nassau is vastly more successful as an international service center than Bridgetown. Part of its success is undoubtedly attributable to its proximity to the mainland of North America. Be that as it may, the city is well established as a primary booking center for offshore banking, and various other sophisticated service subsectors are thriving as well. If New Providence were to become independent of the Bahamas, it would be an excellent example of the successful city-state phenomenon. However, because the island houses the capital of the archipelago nation, the economic prognosis is somewhat altered.

Transportation and communications linkages within the Bahamas have focused attention upon Nassau. Unlike Barbados, where access to Bridgetown can be attained from anywhere in the nation with a modestly priced bus ticket, the decision to go to Nassau from other islands may take on major proportions. In the remote settlements the capital seems far removed. One can estimate the time since the last mail boat by the dwindling stocks in the local food store. Unlike Barbados, the Bahamas seem susceptible to the negative externalities engendered by rural-to-urban migration in larger Third World nations. Life and educational experience gained in remote settlements hardly constitutes what is needed for a successful transition to Nassau's sophisticated service economy. Yet the pull of the capital is seductive as evidenced by the constant flow of inmigrants. Positions with upward mobility are generally beyond the reach of new arrivals, who may find themselves competing for low-paying menial jobs.

What might be classed as the informal sector in Nassau does not provide the survival options that seem to be a population magnet in large Third World cities. In Nassau the bulk of the informal sector, with the exception of illegal activities, has become institutionalized to such an extent that it is hardly informal. The purveyors of straw products and local artifacts rent space in a facility constructed by the government for their express purposes. This facility (straw market) is located in the busiest section of the retail and commercial area, and its tenants have expanded their offerings to include the usual line of souvenirs and paraphernalia to be found in most tourist destinations. At the produce market those who preside over the stalls arrive with their offerings by car from their homes elsewhere on the island. Little seems informal about these forms of business activity. In the poorer areas the usual small sewing and repair shops are to be found. Such enterprises are not the magnet that brings migrants to the capital. The informal sector hardly represents a staging area for such migrants. Thus, when they come, their options are limited and, for subjective reasons, may not include a return to the smaller settlements from whence they came. Thus the Bahamas are hardly an adequate real world example of labor absorption in the neoclassical sense.

If the experiences of Barbados and the Bahamas are a useful bench mark, then the prognosis for many smaller Caribbean jurisdictions seems less than encouraging. Certainly opportunities are limited for small exter-nally oriented urban economies in that region. The success of service centers like the two discussed may preclude similar opportunities in even smaller Caribbean islands. Even common market arrangements involving groups of smaller islands may prove problematical. Such groupings still may not provide the critical mass to allow for import substitution, and the problems of economic integration may be no less difficult than they appear to be in the Bahamas.

The nations discussed to date are the smallest of the small. In larger SINs the neoclassical analysis may prove to be more practical. In the Dominican Republic and Haiti, for example, rural to urban migration more closely resembles patterns that have emerged in larger Third World nations. Jamaica with a population in excess of 2.3 million is also experiencing problems related to rural-to-urban migration. Kingston with a population of somewhat less than 1 million appears to be a smaller edition of the Third World metropolitan prototype, with its informal activities, squatter settlements, and urban underemployment. Even Trinidad's capital, Port of Spain, with a population well below the half-million mark, is experiencing some of the patterns suggested in neoclassical literature. Thus it would appear that the developmental potential of SINs is very different depending on whether they are of the city-state variety, archipelagic, or smaller versions of Third World mainland nations. In all three subgroups it would appear that government expenditures inevitably increase the pressure on urban areas, particularly capital cities, with the result that infrastructure and service needs in other areas go unsatisfied, which in turn increases the pressure on the cities.

In less developed small island states of the Pacific, urbanization poses a development problem, which is especially acute in a number of archipelagic or atoll-based nations, such as the Marshall Islands, Kiribati, and Tuvalu. "While outmigration may solve the immediate problems of some small densely populated atolls, it also may increase the problems of destination areas, especially in atoll states" (Connell, 1986, 50). Connell indicates that some of the South Pacific's most difficult development problems are found in atoll states. "Since aspirations to migrate are much the same in those countries, and infrastructure (principally for health and education) is often highly centralized, migration has been concentrated in a very limited number of areas" (Connell, 1986, 50).

Approximately one-third of the populations of the Marshall Islands, Kiribati, and Tuvalu are respectively concentrated in Majuro, Tarawa, and Funafuti where population densities according to recent censuses have respectively been 1,312; 1,137; and 770 persons per square kilometer. Less than 40% of the population of the Marshall Islands now lives on rural atolls. The Marshall Islands, Kiribati, and Tuvalu all face the problem of depopulation and economic decline of atolls away from the atoll containing the capital city and overurbanization of the principal atoll. Problems in the urban centers include overcrowding, poor housing, increased pollution, unemployment (often disguised), worsened nutrition, increased crime rates, and social disorganization. "These urban problems are not unique to atolls, but the small size of the land and the lagoon areas, and the problems of achieving economic growth accentuate the basic difficulties" (Connell, 1986, 51).

Although a number of factors clearly encourage urbanization and the growth of capital cities at the apparent expense of the rest of the country in small island states in the Pacific, an important factor is the nature of foreign aid. These small economies depend heavily on official foreign aid, which is used mainly to add to government recurrent and capital expenditure. Public administration tends to be centralized and through generated demand, including demand for services, can be a potent force encouraging centralization. Public administration and government work are the main sources of cash employment in the small less developed island nations of the Pacific, and the major proportion of such employment is confined to large urban areas.

It would appear that urbanization has become a major factor in shaping development patterns in small island economies. In the Caribbean region this phenomenon has been characterized in some instances by the emergence of sophisticated service linkages to the world economy. In the South Pacific the urban expansion appears to be relying upon civil service employment as its major economic underpinning. In both the Caribbean and the South Pacific, it seems apparent that urban expansion will continue and that service activities, whether public or private, will contribute the major employment base. To those concerned with the development of such jurisdictions, an understanding of the urban momentum and the forces that it initiates would seem to be basic in solving the problems they face. Certainly that understanding is important if anything is to be done about nonurban development–a serious issue in SINs not cast in the city-state mold.

NOTE

1.   Specific data referring to the Bahamas and Barbados were all extracted from the 1987 report of the Inter-American Development Bank.

7

Migration from and between Small Island Nations

In some SINs of the Third World, population pressures may carry the potential for short circuiting the hopes of those concerned with the overall issue of economic expansion. In this regard it may seem that such jurisdictions are no different from larger emerging nations where population problems have been well documented. If anything it may appear that among smaller nations, especially those of the island variety, scale and environment cooperate in making the overall population issue less acute. Thus in those nations, at least, it may seem that the response to the question, "Will Third World countries be capable of improving the levels of living for their people with the current and anticipated levels of population growth?" (Todaro, 1989, 188) is yes.

Unfortunately smallness is no insurance against the problems of overpopulation. In fact SINs may be facing a dichotomy based upon size. They are too small for modernization to generate the domestic markets that would provide the work opportunities needed to support economic development. Yet increases in their populations may not alleviate that problem; rather rising populations may tax food and other resources thus making the nations in question even more dependent on external linkages and less able to chart their own expansion paths.

Perhaps in some cases SINs could employ external linkages themselves as a means of development. Movements in this direction involving international service activities are becoming increasingly evident. Island ministates are becoming prominent in international finance. Tourism is another service industry seemingly featured in development plans. Manufacturing for export is also a route some developmental efforts are

An earlier version of this chapter appeared as "The Developmental Implications of Migration from and between Small Island Nations" in *International Migration,* Volume 26, Number 4, 1988. Used with permission taking. The types of activities referred to here may all have job creation potential. Some may also contribute needed foreign exchange. Unquestionably, many such activities may have a darker side as well. A taxonomy of such considerations is not the purpose of the current discussion. Instead the focus is on population pressures and more specifically on the role of migration in alleviating those pressures and, hence, in ensuring continued development. The discussion draws on the experience of small nations in the Caribbean Basin and the South Pacific.

The islands of the Caribbean have been experiencing severe population pressures for some time. In some of the smaller islands in what was the British Caribbean, those pressures date from the immediate postslavery era when "little if any land was available for subsistence plots or for truly independent village communities" (Richardson, 1983, 6). According to Richardson some islands, such as St. Kitts, Nevis, Montserrat, Barbados, Grenada, and St. Vincent, looked to migration from that area as a solution to economic problems, and "movement of people back and forth among the small Caribbean islands and beyond continues to the present day" (Richardson, 1983, 6). Richardson sees migration as a tradition, "a mobile livelihood system" that "calls for people to leave, though often to return again, in order to maintain and improve what they had left behind" (Richardson, 1983, 6, referencing Patterson, 1978).

In this century the means of coping with population pressures has been out migration. "Since World War II, some 4.5 million Caribbeans have left the islands and entered the United States" (Lowenthal, 1982, 129). The migration of Cubans and Puerto Ricans to that country is well known. In recent years with the tightening of British immigration regulations with respect to the residents of former colonies, West Indians have turned toward the United States as well. These movements have been characterized as reflecting a "fundamental, continuous, and probably irreversible response to regional overpopulation and the magnetic attraction that any stronger economy exerts on any weaker one" (Lowenthal, 1982, 130).

The position in the Pacific is broadly similar. A high proportion of Micronesians now reside in the United States, and as Connell (1986) states, the Compact of Free Association between various Micronesian states and the United States could result in more Micronesians living in the United States than their home countries. Pacific island countries with a special association with New Zealand, such as the Cook Islands, Niue, and Tokelau, have approximately 50% of their island-born population in New Zealand (Bertram, 1986). From New Zealand members of this immigrant community may reemigrate to Australia because movement between Australia and New Zealand of their citizens is free. The importance of migration as an aspect of the economic operation of these island states has been stressed by Bertram (1986), who develops a special model called the MIRAB model, which includes migration and remittances by migrants as important components. However, not all Pacific island states have migration outlets. For example, this is true of the former British (U.K.) colonies such as Fiji, Kiribati, and Tuvalu. It might also be noted that Australia, unlike New Zealand, has not granted special immigration status to any Pacific island state.

If Lowenthal is correct, his observation reinforces the view of other scholars who have contended "that the distinction between internal and international migration is becoming increasingly artificial" (Butterworth and Chance, 1981, 168). In other words the reasons behind international migration are not substantially different from those prompting the rural exodus that many Third World nations have been experiencing.

The views outlined to date suggest that the basic impetus behind international migration is economic betterment. Of course that motivation is also at work in the case of migrations within Third World nations. However with respect to SINs the current authors suspect that both the causes and the effects of international population movements may be somewhat more difficult to assess than are their counterparts relating to internal migration. Surplus labor in SINs has not been generated in quite the same fashion as in the case of larger Third World nations. Certainly improvements in agricultural technology have played a part as have the declining fortunes of plantation crops in world markets. In this century the terms of trade have turned against agricultural commodities (Nurske, 1967).

Because production for export has always been the aim of plantation economies (Beckford, 1972; 1983), SINs are at risk economically if they have been placing a strong reliance upon that form of agriculture. The term plantation economy has been applied "to those countries of the world where the internal and external dimensions of the plantation system dominate the country's economic, social, and political structure and its relations with the rest of the world" (Beckford, 1983, 12). In such countries it has been suggested that "the plantation system pervades all aspects of life and their development problem must be viewed in this light" (Beckford, 1983, 15).

Beckford recognized that his prognosis applied to most of the Caribbean not to mention "Fiji and certain other islands in the Pacific" as well (Beckford, 1983, 12). What he has suggested would undoubtedly be sufficient to precipitate surplus labor problems in such jurisdictions.

Unfortunately agricultural exports from SINs are facing even more serious problems today. The strictures of the European Common Market have altered agricultural importing practices on the part of its members. Former British colonies, including many from the Caribbean region, are at special risk in this regard. Beyond these difficulties, rising domestic sugar beet production in the United States and the emergence of sugar substitutes have together dealt a serious blow to the fortunes of nations where sugar cane is a major crop.

Certainly the difficulties cited above seem sufficient to restrict the development hopes of SINs where export-oriented agriculture is the basis of the economy. It would appear that the declining fortunes of agricultural commodities in world markets would ensure the emergence of surplus rural labor. This is certainly an issue in some of the smallest Caribbean jurisdictions. In such locations high birth rates and the lack of agricultural opportunities have combined to ensure the emergence of surplus rural labor. In larger Third World nations such rural labor surpluses, however generated, have formed the basis for the rural-to-urban migrations that have been so well documented in the literature of development. In the smallest of island nations, urban survival opportunities may be sparse, seemingly setting the stage for emigration as the strongest option available to those caught in the surplus labor pools.

Beyond the fact that plantation agriculture has fared poorly in the world economy, other factors are at work in the creation of surplus rural labor in SINs. In the Caribbean area plantation economies were based initially on the availability of slave labor. When slavery fell from favor among European nations, some of the colonial economies of the Caribbean switched to a system of indenture to supply the labor needs of their plantations. That expedient was made necessary by the attitude former slave populations had toward plantation work. That attitude has carried into the present in the Caribbean region "where the legacy of slavery has resulted in a high premium being placed on an existence independent of the plantation" (Beckford, 1983, 19). Thus surplus labor has been emerging in various Caribbean nations independent of the international marketing problems of plantation agriculture.

Rural populations alienated from plantations have had to manage on questionable and/or remote land. In the Caribbean region, for example, Barbados, St. Kitts, and Antigua have been faced with a situation whereby little usable land has been available for nonplantation agriculture while Jamaica, Trinidad, and the Windward Islands are examples of jurisdictions where only poor or remote land has been available (Beckford, 1983, 23). All of these interrelated factors recognized by Beckford have contributed to the surplus rural labor problem in the Caribbean quite independent from the usual scenario of improved agricultural technology. Improvements in plantation technology, where they occur, can further complicate the situation as do natural increases in population.

It seems that the forces and attitudes outlined above would combine to generate a pressure to migrate among rural residents of SINs. Certainly some evidence of this is apparent in the Caribbean Basin region. In Puerto Rico, which holds a unique relationship to the United States, cities have been growing as a direct result of in migration from rural areas. In Jamaica the Kingston area has been experiencing population and labor absorption problems more characteristic of larger Third World metropolitan complexes. In Haiti the plight of the rural peasantry has reached crisis proportions. Among the smaller SINs in the Caribbean, the rural-to-urban drift of surplus population has had fewer visible results, or perhaps the smallness of the jurisdictions in question understates the seriousness of population pressures.

Population surpluses appear to originate in rural areas, but little evidence suggests that those surpluses are the basis for long established and continuing emigration patterns involving the SINs of the Caribbean Basin region. Thus the view exposed earlier in this discussion to the effect that there is little difference between rural-to-urban and international migration may be an oversimplification, as may be the concept that emigration is the solution for population problems among SINs. Writing in 1985, Robert A. Pastor raised doubts about emigration being as useful an ingredient in the developmental plans of Caribbean nations as may have been previously supposed (Pastor, 1985, 14–15). In support of his position, he suggested that the average Caribbean migrant has more education, better health, and earns a higher income than typical countrymen. "Most migrants were employed until the time of their departure" and "many islands are exporting highly motivated labor with scarce skills" (Pastor, 1985, 14). If Pastor is correct, emigration parts company with rural-to-urban migration as a response to the emergence of surplus labor. When ambitious skilled workers leave the country, their actions have little to do with the existence of domestic surplus labor and their leaving may do little to facilitate domestic labor absorption. Pastor was undoubtedly aware of this. His discussion implies that the type of out migration that has been occurring in the Caribbean is contributing little to economic development.

It seems clear that emigration and population movements internal to SINs involve dissimilar population groups and have differing effects upon developmental processes. The emergence of surplus labor described earlier is a phenomenon that is widespread throughout the Third World.

Although the causes of this emerging surplus may differ in the case of various SINs in the Caribbean, from what seems typical of larger Third World nations, the policy implications are all too familiar. If such ministates wish to sustain their hopes of economic expansion, they must find the means to employ their surplus labor. Such small jurisdictions may not have survival options available in their urban informal sectors, nor is it likely that the unemployed can find jobs in manufacturing processes generated through import substitution strategies. The seriousness of this problem is manifest in the time it takes young people to be absorbed into working populations in even the most menial capacities.

Despite the traditional reliance upon emigration in the face of population problems, a downside to that strategy has become clear (Pastor, 1985). The migrants most acceptable to advanced nations possess skills, and their departure leaves gaps in the labor forces of SINs. These gaps are not easily filled from the ranks of surplus labor. Their going, if it retards modern sector activities, may actually slow development and retard opportunities for labor absorption.

Those in the unskilled surplus labor pools are not as attractive as potential emigrants to advanced nations, witness the continuing saga of the Haitians in their attempts to seek better lives in the Bahamas, much less the United States. In the Caribbean Basin the plight of those in the surplus labor pools who choose to leave their homelands is often that of the illegal alien. When such persons move between islands or jurisdictions, they may well complicate the labor situation in their new host territory, and/or they may be exploited in the labor markets of such jurisdictions. Haitian populations have been developing in various locations in the French Antilles despite the fact that those jurisdictions have surplus labor problems of their own. Barbados and Trinidad have been experiencing in migration, often of an illegal nature from the smaller islands of the southeastern Caribbean. The U.S. Virgin Islands have become an attractive destination for émigrés from northeastern Caribbean islands.

Population movements internal to the Caribbean region have the potential for further complicating surplus labor and/or population problems. They may lead to draconian travel regulations aimed at keeping out unwanted surplus manpower, or in more permissive circumstances, to the exploitation of unskilled migrants. At a recent academic conference held in Guadeloupe, various presentations were cancelled because their authors had not met rather stringent visa requirements. The visa requirements in question probably were not aimed at those whom they impacted. Nonetheless, stringent travel restrictions, even where justified, may interfere with legitimate commercial or cultural exchanges, perhaps to the detriment of the developmental objectives of the countries or jurisdictions concerned.

If protective entry requirements impede normal interisland relations, it is quite possible that they may interfere with developmental processes. Such practices probably will cause retaliatory measures. Even without such retaliation they make the interisland business climate less conducive to development. If the illegal immigration that some SINs and other territories in the Caribbean are experiencing is the result of the informal extension of documented visits, it is possible that more stringent entry requirements may stem the flow of illegal aliens. Unfortunately the realities of informal migration in the Caribbean are somewhat more complicated because the migrants in question do not necessarily arrive through ports of entry. Such new arrivals are unaccounted for from the start. Unlike formal migrants to metropolitan nations, they are less likely to have special skills to offer. Thus they further complicate surplus labor and population problems in the jurisdictions they enter. As such complications become evident, the result may be a further tightening of general interisland travel requirements and consequent constraints upon regional economic integration. The implications of this scenario with respect to development potential are both evident and unfortunate.

The interisland movement of unskilled labor, whether legal or illegal, may lead to the scenario explained by W. Arthur Lewis in relation to rural-to-urban migration. The purpose behind the interisland movement of unskilled surplus labor may well be survival. That being the case, such migrations will continue as long as participants in them can expect employment at subsistence wages at the end of their journey. A flow of such workers will, of course, hold down unskilled wages in recipient territories, thus ensuring a doubtful economic plight for unskilled workers in the domestic population. This type of international migration is similar in some respects to the continuing rural-to-urban flow in Third World nations and quite distinct from the movement of more skilled labor to metropolitan nations.

The movement of unskilled labor between jurisdictions, whether legal or illegal, may have serious repercussions for the workers concerned. This point is well illustrated by recent experiences involving Haitian workers. During the regime of Jean-Claude Duvalier, arrangements were made for Haitians to work in the sugar industry of the Dominican Republic. The workers in question became trapped in adverse circumstances, which have been well documented (Lemoine, 1981). It is doubtful that their presence in the Dominican Republic has contributed much to broadening development in that country. If anything, it has served to depress wages among the least skilled members of the nation's labor force. Aside from their physical removal from the Haitian labor force, it is doubtful that their departure contributed to the development potential of that nation. The circumstances of their employment were such as to preclude remittances, to a substantial extent, thus removing what has been recognized in many Caribbean jurisdictions as a very positive offshoot from emigration.

The illegal entry of Haitians into the Bahamas has produced equally questionable results. That country has experienced a substantial influx in recent years, an understandable occurrence in the light of Haiti's geographical proximity. In the Bahamas, Haitians have appeared in urban areas where they have assumed the most menial occupations. They have also appeared in more remote locations where they can be found performing field work and/or menial tasks related to tourism.

As a nation the Bahamas may be more fortunate than many of the small nations of the Caribbean region. As has been recognized in the case of the encroachment of illegal aliens in the labor markets of the United States, it might be suggested that Haitians are not taking jobs either needed or wanted by Bahamians. Anecdotal evidence supports that contention, yet internal migration patterns in the Bahamas suggest that that nation possesses labor absorption problems of its own.

In general it would seem that migration is hardly a feasible strategy of population control for SINs in the modern world. The long relied on escape valve of metropolitan nations is not so readily available today. Emigration to such destinations has become much more complicated. Some advanced nations have for all practical purposes stopped such population movements, and others have imposed quotas. The new stringency in metropolitan immigration seems to ensure that the bulk of those accepted possess employable skills. As has been mentioned above, the departure of such persons from the workforce of SINs may not speed further labor absorption in such locations and may, in fact, weaken the quality of the labor force and, thus, retard development. It should be noted that the types of skills referred to here are not those normally classed as the "brain drain."

If migration of a permanent nature appears to be an impractical solution for the surplus labor problems of SINs, a temporary form of migration may be capable of a more positive contribution to the development hopes of such jurisdictions. In the Caribbean region there has been a tradition of temporary foreign employment. Workers from various island jurisdictions made a considerable contribution to the construction of the Panama Canal. American held sugar estates in Cuba and the Dominican

Republic received considerable help from workers recruited in Haiti, Jamaica, and other islands during the first three decades of this century (Richardson, 1983, 21). Early in this century many short-term laboring jobs available in Bermuda were filled by workers from the Caribbean (Richardson, 1983, 18-22). At present both Canada and the United States have ongoing temporary worker programs, which rely upon various Caribbean jurisdictions to supply labor for their harvests. The burgeoning cruise industry relies heavily upon workers from Third World sources, and, with the large concentration of that industry in the Caribbean Basin, some of its workers are recruited from that region.

Although temporary foreign employment can foster problems of exploitation, this form of going abroad seems to have a more realistic potential for positive impacts in SINs than the forms of migration discussed above. Workers going abroad under such circumstances may send back remittances to relatives. When they return, they may do so with a small financial stake, which may aid them in establishing a more secure future. Even temporary absences take some pressure away from local labor markets.

Temporary migration can also impose significant economic costs on the source country. Temporary migrants are frequently the most productive and enterprising individuals, and they are lost to their own economy usually during their most productive years. Consequently, their potential contribution to the development of their home country may be lost. In addition social problems can develop because males are most often temporary migrants and leave females, children, and older family members behind to cope as best they can. The social cohesion and productivity of the family unit can be seriously impaired. Permanent migration more commonly involves the migration of whole families or substantial fractions of them, either in the first instance or eventually.

Furthermore, temporary migration may result in the source country being unable to capitalize on its initial investment in training and education of temporary migrants. Their return to their home country toward the end of their working life may also impose an economic burden on their home country. From this time on they are likely to become increasingly dependent on others for economic support. Many developed countries, however, are more receptive to temporary migration than to permanent migration from SINs.

Temporary migration is hardly the solution to development and overpopulation problems facing island ministates. If such jurisdictions are to improve their material situations, more economic cooperation among them will be required. More attention will have to be given to effective linkages with the world economy. It would seem that import substitution through cooperation among SINs, production for export where feasible, and more attention to more sophisticated international service linkages hold a better prospect for material progress than merely relying on exporting surplus populations.

8

Some Specifics on Education and the Brain Drain

Commenting on education in his classic text, W. Arthur Lewis observed, "The difficulty education raises is that it is both a consumer and an investment service." That observation, although more than 30 years old, is relevant for Third World policy makers in the 1990s. Elaborating on his remark, Lewis suggested, "The difficulty is where to draw the line with those types of education which contribute more to enjoyment than to output — literacy for example." According to Lewis, "In economic terms, such part of education as is not a profitable investment is on a par with other consumer goods" (Lewis, 1954, 183). There is little doubt that a thorough understanding of the Lewis position, as summarized here, would be of considerable assistance to policy makers who are struggling with educational priorities in small island economies.

Writing in 1975, Fritz Machlup suggested that "we must understand the solicitudes of legislators and administrators in charge of appropriating scarce resources, wanting to show that most of the funds channeled into education are used not just for 'luxuries' but for social investment yielding high returns to society" (Machlup, 1975, 22). Machlup illustrated how education can at times "be a hinderance instead of a help to economic efficiency" (Machlup, 1975, 23). He suggested that primary education may interfere with growth in agricultural societies "where the 'educated' refuse to work in agriculture but cannot be absorbed into industry" (Machlup, 1975, 23). This observation seems disturbingly relevant to various small island economies in the Caribbean region.

The observation is also relevant to the South Pacific islands, but participation in education in these islands is relatively low with enrollments declining rapidly after primary school (Joint Committee on Foreign Affairs, Defence and Trade, 1989, 82–83). Indeed, school enrollments in the Solomon Islands and Vanuatu are among the lowest in the world, and they probably come close to satisfying Machlup's suggested participation pattern.

Going beyond his reservation concerning primary education, Machlup observed "that secondary and higher education may lead to aversion to manual work, while opportunities for nonmanual work are lacking" (Machlup, 1975, 23). Other economists have recognized that "it clearly cannot be assumed that the link between education and economic growth is a direct and linear one, or that it operates in the same manner for every kind of society" (Fagerlind and Saha, 1983, 76). Fagerlind and Saha are careful to point out that educational investments are costly to the extent that they take funds away from other economic or social projects. Problems relating to the appropriateness of educational expenditures do not appear to end with opportunity costs. "The increasing levels of unemployment in most countries, which in recent years has paralleled educational expansion, suggests a certain inappropriateness of a certain kind of schooling during periods of educational and social change" (Fagerlind and Saha, 1983, 77).

Those authors suggest some fine tuning for the educational offerings of poorer societies with an emphasis "on primary and some secondary education with a careful selection of vocationally-oriented subjects" (Fagerlind and Saha, 1983, 88–89). Machlup was much more definite in his recommendations: "Instead of aiming at social justice in providing schooling for all, a poor country does much better in having only one-fifth or even less of its children go to primary school, but providing secondary education for some of the more talented" (Machlup, 1975, 25). Machlup's position cannot be easily dismissed as mere educational ideology. In defense of his policy of providing more years of education to fewer students, he argues that high enrollments in lower grades are uneconomic where dropout rates are high. Instead he suggested, "Secondary and vocational education for the most teachable graduates of primary school has paid off very well for most developing countries" (Machlup, 1975, 25).

In the South Pacific islands, Australia has given considerable foreign aid for the development of education. The educational structure that has emerged in many of these countries is one in which a large share of the support goes to relatively few students to continue their education to tertiary level. In many ways, the structure has similarities with that suggested by Machlup, but it is not as vocationally oriented. In this respect a recent Australian enquiry concluded:

Despite this program of assistance, and the involvement of other donors, the Committee is disturbed at the continued inadequacy of primary and secondary education in the region, and questions whether Australia has placed too great an emphasis on the tertiary sector rather than upgrading primary and secondary levels. The Committee is also concerned about large infrastructural projects that appear to have dominated educational aid to the region (Joint Committee on Foreign Affairs, Defence and Trade, 1989, 84).

Problems noted in education in the South Pacific islands include shortages of textbooks and learning aids, short supplies of schools and school buildings, underqualified teachers, lack of qualified and experienced educational administrators, and uneconomic teacher training programs. These are problems in most developing countries. Other problems include the scattered nature of the archipelagoes, which make it difficult on some of the smaller islands to provide economically anything other than basic education (cf., Conroy, 1982, Ch. 4). At higher levels of education, students must proceed to study at more central places involving extra costs and disrupting family life. While distance education can overcome these difficulties to some extent, it is by no means a complete and perfect solution, especially at tertiary level (Anon, 1986).

Despite the intuitions of economists dating back to the 1950s, according to Michael Todaro, "Most Third World nations have been led to believe or have wanted to believe that it is the rapid quantitative expansion of educational opportunities that holds the key to national development" (Todaro, 1989, 330). This belief system Todaro felt was until recently so strongly held as to defy any serious challenge. Few would dispute the contention that education has a vital role to play in any scenario involving economic development. However, it is also becoming quite clear that education is no panacea for the problems of development and, more specifically, for problems relating to labor absorption and growth in the modern sector. The belief that education on its own is a key to the job markets of the modern sector and, hence, to a better life stems from observations relating to job markets in developed economies. If realistic educational policies are to be developed in Third World nations, major adjustments in preconceptions and wish lists will be required. Such adjustments may be particularly pertinent to the needs of small island economies.

Preconceptions and misperceptions about the role of education may be present in donor countries as well as Third World countries. In relation to education and Australian aid for education in the South Pacific, an Australian Parliamentary Committee recently stated:

Education, human resource development, is vitally important to the development process of any society. Skilled people are essential in both the public and private sectors to sustain, manage and capitalize on progress in development. Australia has recognized the central role of education in sustaining moves towards development and in achieving self-sufficiency in administrative, managerial and technological expertise [and education is a major part of its foreign aid program] (Joint Committee on Foreign Affairs, Defence and Trade, 1989, 81).

In practice, views and findings of economists about the role of education in economic development are mixed (Levin, 1989). While some researchers believe that the return on expenditure on education is high in developing countries (education being considered as a capital investment in humans), others are unconvinced (Psacharopoulos, 1973; 1984; Schultz, 1960; 1961; Blaug, 1976). Educational investment is positively correlated with economic growth and levels of per capita income, but it may be to a large extent a consequence of these rather than a causal agent. The problem is that there is interdependence rather than simple dependence of economic growth and per capita income levels on educational expenditure. Furthermore, it is apparent that returns on educational investment depend upon the presence of suitable complementary resources and economic opportunities for the educated. If these complementary factors of production are limited, as they are likely to be in SINs, returns on educational investment may be low. This may be true notwithstanding the fact that improvements in the quality of factors of production (labor and capital) have been a major contributor to economic growth in some developed countries (Denison, 1962).

As indicated previously, education is not solely undertaken as a productive investment even though the investment aspect is stressed in the human capital approach (Becker, 1975). It may be undertaken partially for consumption purposes. Furthermore, the education system acts as a filtering or screening device and may help to select individuals with particular characteristics, e.g., intelligence or persistence in intellectual tasks. Up to a point this can be of economic value, but, if the system is heavily subsidized by governments, there may be excessive investment in the sorting process. Because of the subsidy, individuals may persist longer in the educational system to ensure selection for the type of job they have in mind. However, the accuracy of matching individuals and jobs may increase only marginally, and the extra benefits to society are likely to be less than the extra cost if the filtering process is made too fine (Arrow, 1973; Spence, 1973). Because developing countries, especially SINs, are short of capital resources, they can ill afford to invest in uneconomic sorting systems based on the educational process but may nevertheless do so if they try to replicate the systems of more developed countries.

Some writers argue that educational systems tend to reinforce existing social stratifications because the children of existing leading classes are more likely to gain access to educational resources and succeed. In studies of school children in Papua New Guinea, Conroy (1982, Ch. 6) found that they perceived education to be important in terms of payoff through money income, prestige, and power. In traditional Melanesian societies behavior is strongly directed to achieving status and prestige, and these may be much more important than the economic value of the behavior in itself. This may help to explain why colonial forms of education have persisted in many developing countries — they are associated with power and prestige. In Zimbabwe, for instance, the educational system has changed little since independence, but the ruling black elite is now increasingly sending its children to schools that were once the preserves of whites (Edwards and Tisdell, 1988). In most developing countries, including those in the South Pacific, the degree of subsidy for education tends to rise with the level of education, being highest at tertiary level. This pattern tends to favor existing elites, given that their children are more likely to remain in the educational system to higher levels.

Nevertheless, empirical evidence suggests that greater participation in education and widespread improvements in the quality of the population can be powerful forces in reducing inequality of income (Gillis et al., 1983, 83; Ahluwalia, 1976). Yet it is unclear that the effect is a simple causal one. Furthermore, those who favor the basic human needs approach to education tend to emphasize that basic universal education is an important precursor to economic growth and that the education of women can play an important role in improving family health. In many societies, including several in the South Pacific, women are responsible for much production at the subsistence level, so the impact of their education on productivity should also be considered.

Many small island economies in the Caribbean region are facing a dichotomy in population dynamics. They are threatened by overpopulation yet lack the population thresholds required to build strong local markets. Issues related to population have always been a concern in the Caribbean. "Prosperity was initially dependent upon imported slave labor and later upon indentured labor from India and the Orient" (McKee, 1983b, 58). In recent years, however, the region has been characterized by rising populations and consequent labor absorption problems. No evidence shows that improvements in education have lessened the surplus labor problem.

In the Pacific islands, rising education levels have occurred together with rising unemployment rates especially for the young. According to Browne and Scott (1989), it has been impossible to absorb growing labor supplies into the formal economy. Nevertheless, rapid growth in real wages of those employed (mostly in the government sector) has occurred, and high rates of unemployment are present.

Writing in 1979, Malcolm Cross suggested, "Advances in educational attainment between generations naturally mean that the unemployed tend to be better educated than the employed" (Cross, 1979, 54). Cross found it disturbing that chronic employment and underemployment difficulties affecting the young in both rural and urban settings did not "appear to be on the way to solution with advances in industrialization" (Cross, 1979, 54). As has already been discussed in the present volume, the method of choice for diffusing population pressures and presumably unemployment problems has been out migration (Chapter 8).

In a region where out migration may have been close to achieving a policy position, it would have been surprising if the phenomenon known throughout the Third World as the brain drain had not emerged. Emigration has certainly emerged as the perceived solution for individuals caught in the difficulties of survival and/or personal advancement. "Generally speaking out migrants tend to be better educated than those left behind, since a successful move requires the possession of an employable skill" (McKee, 1985, 58).

If out migration is to be relied upon as a population control, a dichotomy emerges in education policy. Among workers migrating from certain Caribbean jurisdictions to the United States between 1962 and 1976, five groups stood out numerically: "professional, technical, and kindred workers (PTK); clerical and kindred workers; craftsmen, foremen, and kindred workers; operative and kindred workers; and private household workers" (Palmer, 1979, 93). Of his five categories Palmer went on to identify four as "crucial in terms of the loss of skilled workers, since they represent people with years of formal and on-the-job training, a cost borne by the sending country" (Palmer, 1979, 94). Herein lies the dichotomy for education policy makers. Presumably, various types of skilled labor are required by nations who hope to improve their material status. By adjusting resources available for education to ensure the basic training needed to supply the skills in question, the policy makers may be removing the barriers separating their trainees from international labor markets. Even in jurisdictions with a surplus of well-trained labor, the strongest subcohorts of skilled workers will be most likely to emigrate. To the extent that such emigration occurs, the root jurisdictions are not simply losing skilled labor, they are absorbing the training costs of labor acquired by foreign, and generally, more developed nations.

According to Edward Seaga, former Prime Minister of Jamaica, that country lost roughly 60% of its professional graduates to North America during the period 1977–80 (Dowty, 1986, 158). Earlier evidence from Jamaica reveals a similar pattern. For the years 1973–1974 "The highest rate of emigration is clearly from the incremental output of medical doctors, followed by accountants, engineers, and nurses" (Palmer, 1979, 95). According to Palmer, Trinidad has also experienced difficulties with respect to the migration of skilled manpower and recognized this phenomenon in its Third Five-Year Plan 1967–1973 "as a threat to its development effort" (Palmer, 1979, 96). In a recent more general discussion of the brain drain, it has been suggested that the "bulk of Third World emigrant professionals come from a few nations" and that in Latin America the Caribbean nations are among the major losers (Dowty, 1986, 164). Dowty goes on to suggest, "What most of these countries have in common is a large population base and a relatively advanced educational system, especially in relation to the professional opportunities available" (Dowty, 1986, 164).

Although the island economies of the Caribbean Basin are quite small, they tend to be overpopulated and by and large do enjoy rather strong educational systems. This is especially true of the English-speaking jurisdictions, where the language itself reinforces the educational system in preparing potential entrants to labor markets in the United States. Dowty provides at least an implicit insight into the situation facing the more developed Caribbean islands with respect to the loss of trained workers. "Countries at a higher level of development seem to have more trouble, apparently because of imbalances between education and opportunities available" (Dowty, 1986, 165).

The impact of the brain drain on the more advanced nations of the region may be arguable, but Haiti, which is one of the poorest nations in the Western Hemisphere, suffered ongoing losses of trained personnel throughout the Duvalier years. Dowty cites the Haitian situation as, in all probability, the "most intensive and systematic brain drain in the world" encompassing 60% to 75% of the nation's high-level workforce since 1950 (Dowty, 1986, 165). Thus it would appear that small island economies in the Caribbean, at various levels of development, are experiencing a loss of trained personnel.

Although Dowty acknowledged noneconomic motivations for professional emigration from Third World nations, he seems to have been convinced that "the decisive motivation appears to be one of working conditions and employment" (Dowty, 1986, 165). He emphasized the lack of suitable jobs as the main causal factor behind the loss of professionals from Third World nations and was careful to suggest that "it is not the availability of more tempting options in the developed world that is at the core of the problem" (Dowty, 1986, 166).

Survey research involving scientific personnel from Latin America and the Caribbean region, who were working in the United States, would seem to suggest that Dowty's view of the situation may be somewhat oversimplified. In parallel studies of expatriate scientists from the Andean Pact nations, a selection of Caribbean nations, and Argentina, educational considerations were clearly the most important factor motivating the decision to migrate (McKee, 1983a; 1983b; 1985). The acquisition of professional credentials from U.S. institutions of higher learning provided an entry into that nation's scientific job markets, and the university experiences themselves, no doubt, contributed to a smooth cultural transition.

Of 40 respondents from nations of the Commonwealth Caribbean, "twenty-five cited educational considerations as their major reason for entering the country. . . . In eight . . . cases the decision was work oriented" (McKee, 1983b, 62). In addition to ranking by the respondents, the importance of educational considerations can also be seen in the pattern of degrees acquired. The study identified only three respondents who had received their Bachelor's degree from their homeland and none who had received advanced degrees. At the doctoral level 31 hold U.S. degrees, and 8 hold degrees from other nations (McKee, 1983b, 62). As suggested by the study, the risk of losing skilled manpower is increased if foreign educational institutions are relied upon for higher education.

It may be that certain small island jurisdictions lack the diversity of job opportunities to regain their nationals who have acquired specialized expertise through study abroad. That is a somewhat different causal circumstance than that espoused by Dowty when he suggested that the lack of suitable jobs was the main factor for losing professionals from Third World nations. A shortage of opportunities may keep away some who had other reasons. Dowty appears to be philosophical about such losses in any case "since a professional who remained at home would probably not find employment by making use of his skills, and his presence would not speed development" (Dowty, 1986, 166).

Without dwelling too long about whether professionals migrate or migrants become professionals who then cannot return home, suffice it to say that Dowty is undoubtedly correct in thinking that professional opportunities are not as plentiful in the Third World as they are in more developed economies. When he suggests that countries with the greatest outflow of professionals are not necessarily "hurting" more, as they are in no position to use the lost skills anyway, he is also correct. Expatriate nuclear engineers from SINs are not depriving those jurisdictions of a nuclear power industry. Such an industry is probably not needed. The same is undoubtedly true of a variety of professionals and specialists and the industries they service.

The major loss suffered by SINs when their nationals assume professional responsibilities elsewhere is not the skills these former residents have acquired but the tasks they might have performed had they sought careers more in line with the needs of their homelands. Larger Third World nations may have a broader potential for using skills similar to those acquired by their expatriates, and for such jurisdictions the brain drain presents a different set of issues. Among SINs the major threat from the brain drain stems from the loss of their brightest young citizens sufficient to generate debilitating results with respect to their overall developmental efforts or national well-being.

Dowty cites the brain drain as an index of the inability of the Third World to compete with developed nations and as a symbol of gains the latter have realized at the expense of the Third World (Dowty, 1986, 168). In the case of small island economies, such symbolism may have little meaning. The policy implications of such a negative symbiosis should have more to do with structuring domestic educational systems to ensure that local manpower needs are met than with measures to combat the brain drain, much less recoup real or imputed losses from it.

In small island jurisdictions with severe population pressures and consequent labor absorption difficulties, it might be less than facetious to suggest that the continuing out migration of trained personnel is not necessarily something to be stopped. The observation, alluded to earlier, by Malcolm Cross concerning the Caribbean area comes to mind: "Advances in educational attainment between generations naturally mean that the unemployed tend to be better educated than the employed" (Cross, 1979, 54). Since Great Britain adopted restrictive immigration practices in 1962, the former British possessions in the Caribbean have not had the luxury of population control through substantial out migration. In a much more competitive climate for the export of surplus population, the level of education among prospective out migrants may be an important selling point. The provision of education could even be recommended as a plank in a policy of population control, assuming that the skill-needs of domestic labor markets are being met simultaneously. In such jurisdictions concerns over the brain drain may appear to be more theoretical than practical. If skilled workers, by finding work abroad are relieving population pressures and if the specialized skills of expatriates are not needed in their home countries, that governments pay little more than lip service to the supposed problem of the brain drain is hardly surprising.

Scope for international migration by Pacific islanders appears to be more limited than in the Caribbean, and the issue of the brain drain does not appear overall to have been a major one for them. The main leakage is to New Zealand from the limited number of islands for which it permits relatively free migration, namely Niue, Tokelau, and the Cook Islands, and there is some leakage to the United States from American Samoa. Furthermore, with the Compact of Free Association, the migration drain from the Marshall Islands to the United States can be expected to increase. Australia does not provide any particular concessions for accepting South Sea islanders as migrants. They must qualify under the same conditions as everyone else, which in practice means that it is very difficult for South Sea islanders to gain entry to Australia. Thus the ratio of such immigrants to Australia to the total Australian intake of immigrants is relatively low (Joint Committee on Foreign Affairs, Defence and Trade, 1989, Ch. 6).

Lip service notwithstanding, the existence of the brain drain indicates an international market for professional personnel, the existence of which may have further implications for nations throughout the Third World. To find acceptance in the international markets for professional skills, job seekers must conform to the accrediting processes of those markets. They must acquire the training and the credentials required. Internationally homogeneous professional credentials should be of concern to the Third World because there is no guarantee that experts armed with them will have the type of training required to deal with the specific needs of emerging nations.

International licensing and accrediting procedures often produce medical practitioners and other professionals equipped to deal with the needs of developed nations. This may solidify the effect of the brain drain if professionals trained abroad find their skills do not match the needs of their homelands. Unfortunately, problems associated with international training and licensing procedures do not end on this note. Responding to a survey, one Trinidadian professional residing in the United States found "too great a belief in the superiority of foreign professionals on the part of politicians . . . although academic background of foreign professionals is no better and local professionals have advantage of better knowledge of local customs, materials, needs, etc." (McKee, 1983b,

65). This phenomenon brings cadres of consultants and expatriate professional personnel to Third World nations. In SINs the use of such practitioners may result in the total elimination of domestic professionals from some fields, regardless of where they may have been trained.

Problems do not cease with the elimination of professional opportunities for domestic personnel. Discussing the brain drain in his widely used text, Todaro suggests that it "has not merely reduced the supply of vital professional people available within developing countries . . . it has diverted the attention of those scientists, doctors, architects, engineers, and academics who remain from important local problems and goals" (Todaro, 1989, 353). Todaro suggests that perceptions of what should be done, and how, permeates virtually all facets of professional practice, quite possibly having serious impacts on development goals and projects designed to achieve them. He sees skilled professionals "dominated by rich country ideas as to what represents true professional excellence" and suggests they "migrate intellectually" and contribute to what he terms an internal brain drain (Todaro, 1989, 353). Todaro's remarks appear to be especially relevant to small island economies. Jurisdictions in the Caribbean may well be at special risk because of strong demonstration effects from the mainland of North America.

The policy implications of the brain drain and general educational considerations are intertwined in SINs. If economic progress is to occur in such jurisdictions, their educational systems must reflect local needs at all levels. Those needs may vary from island to island in keeping with the nature of local economies. Thus, on the one hand, plantation economies may do well to heed Machlup's cautions concerning too much primary education (Machlup, 1975, 23). On the other hand, island economies based upon tourism and other service industries will have more need of a literate labor pool.

Certainly it would appear that vocational education at the secondary level would benefit most small island economies. In some instances island economies could benefit from efforts to ensure that traditional skills, which have been passed down from generation to generation through informal instruction and on-the-job training, continue to be nurtured. In the northeastern Caribbean efforts are under way to identify traditional products, with an eye to reviving or retaining markets for them (Kemp, 1987, 3, 6). In some small island economies, such efforts are important not just for the very useful items produced but also for their role in providing jobs on a continuing basis, thus retarding surplus labor problems.

In the South Pacific, the education system is less vocationally oriented than may seem desirable. Professor Helen Hughes argued recently that the education system in the South Pacific has become increasingly inappropriate to the needs of the people and too closely akin to the British academic model. She has advocated more technical training and vocationally oriented training (Joint Committee on Foreign Affairs, Defence and Trade, 1989, 85). To a large extent the school and education system in Oceania is a legacy of an earlier colonial status and neocolonial influences (Thomas and Postlethwaite, 1984).

Primary and secondary curricula, which have been preserved intact from colonial times or which simply replicate programs in advanced nations, may prepare surplus population for emigration but may do little to supply the labor skills needed in the domestic economy. The accumulation of literate, unemployed labor pools, which are evident in some Caribbean economies, may simply be a function of populations that are growing too rapidly. Such pools may also suggest too much money spent on education in general or even the inappropriate nature of existing educational offerings.

In SINs that enjoy university facilities, the opportunity exists to target educational offerings to the needs of the domestic economy or, at least, to the needs of various economies in the same general region. Following such a policy would contribute appreciably to reducing the potential for negative impacts from the brain drain. Sound policy apparently requires that education at all levels be regarded as a delivery system for needed human capital and that, in jurisdictions where human capital needs are not being met, adjustments in educational offerings are indicated.

9

Criminal Activity and Development

Criminal activity is included in the current discussions to provide an assessment of its impact on the development of the jurisdictions under consideration. For that reason the discussion may take a somewhat different direction than have works on the economic impact of crime in larger, more developed economies.

Writing in 1984, Klaus de Albuquerque summarized earlier research findings that he felt were pertinent to the study of crime in developing countries (de Albuquerque, 1984, 94). Among the findings cited was the contention that "rising crime incidence is generally associated with socio-economic development and more specifically with urbanization and industrialization." Clinard and Abbot (1973) claim that one of the reasons increasing crime is associated with urbanization in developing countries is that transition of the migrant from rural areas to an urban one involves one sharp leap rather than gradual change through intermediate stages, as in the history of the developed world. Thus the migrant in a developing country is faced with immediate economic stress and an identity problem and runs the hazard of engaging in crime or prostitution (see also Clinard, 1976).

Another feature of Third World crime was the dominance of young males as perpetrators. The crimes committed were mainly "property related, involving for the most part thefts of high demand consumer durables" although "the escalation in property crime is followed by a rising incidence of crimes against persons" (de Albuquerque, 1984, 94). Whether this overview of Third World activity fits circumstances in small island economies remains to be seen. It may not form the basis of an understanding suited to public policy formulation in such jurisdictions, if the policies are to reflect the needs of economic expansion. "The Caribbean has historically had fairly high violent crime rates (above those of most developing regions)" and "Caribbean countries lead other developing nations" in the incidence of both drug-related and property offenses (de Albuquerque, 1984, 97).

Economists seem to regard most criminal behavior as rational (Anderson, 1976). "In contrast to biological, sociological and psychological theories, the economic theory of crime views the criminal as possessing a motivation that is the same as that of the noncriminal. That is, rational behavior rather than deviant or abnormal behavior is the basis underlying a criminal's decision to undertake illegal activities" (Lin and Loeb, 1980, 25). In another context economists have described criminal behavior "as a case of human behavior under the condition of uncertainty" (Luksetich and White, 1982, 2). The essence of their argument was that the decision to commit a crime on the individual level involves adopting a course of action expected to yield the greatest benefits relative to potential costs. This point of view introduces the criminal as a subspecies of economic man, who elects his or her actions in pursuit of maximum personal satisfaction.

It is doubtful that individual criminal decisions are made any differently in Third World settings, although a portion of the individual's personal utility calculus may revolve around minimal survival options. Because the current discussion is not concerned directly with the real or presumed relationship between crime and poverty, the notion of crime as an individual survival option will not be pursued directly except where the acts perpetrated in pursuit of survival have direct effects upon development.

As in all societies, policy makers in Third World economies, and certainly in small island jurisdictions, are faced with formulating programs to deal with crime. Economists have recognized costs as a major component of the decision-making processes relating to law enforcement (Hellman, 1980, 55 ff.; and Luksetich and White, 1982, 180 ff.). More specifically they have been concerned with "recognizing the ways in which criminal activity hurts society" and, thus, with the amount that should be spent on crime prevention (Hellman, 1980, 55).

The specifics of determining anticrime budgets and the programs they support undoubtedly face more serious constraints in Third World settings than is the case in more prosperous nations. In small island economies expenditures related to crime must compete for their position in public policy pecking orders, with the general needs of development, not to mention the programs all governments seem expected to provide. However, in the case of small island economies, the success of this competition and the capabilities of such jurisdictions in dealing with crime-related problems are severely constrained by the realities of public funding shortfalls.

All economies in electing to spend public funds on matters related to crime may preclude certain other public services, so social opportunity costs are involved in all such decisions. In electing to fight crime SINs may be forced to forgo other needs. In the case of projects directly related to economic development, the trade-offs with law enforcement and crime prevention may be severe. That being the case it is generally impractical for Third World policy makers to strive to totally eliminate criminal activity. In this regard their options may appear to differ only in degree from those of similar policy makers in wealthier nations. Despite the ideal of a crime free society, economists and other social scientists concerned with crime-related issues agree that the practical policy objective should be to keep the incidence and, thus, the negative overspill from crime within tolerable bounds. The setting of such limits will always involve the assessment of the opportunity costs incurred by the menu of anticriminal practices elected.

Third World nations may rationally allow higher levels of criminal activity than are tolerated in wealthier nations. This would be in keeping with the efficient allocation of public financial resources across the entire spectrum of public needs. Faced with such allocation decisions, Third World nations may be forced to establish pecking orders of criminal activities to be eliminated, reduced, or tolerated based upon the perceived impact that each activity in question may have upon the society's goals and priorities.

Those who study criminal activity often subdivide it according to whether it involves persons or property. A third subcategory includes so-called victimless crimes. In most societies, public sentiment would give priority to contain violent crimes, particularly those directed at people. By contrast the need to allocate public funds toward prevention or control of the so-called victimless crimes is often given least importance. In Third World settings little suggests that public sentiment would differ substantially from this pattern.

This similarity of public sentiment in advanced economies and Third World settings need not necessarily support a case for parallel public policy pecking orders. The scarcity of funds and developmental needs may order substantial differences in the priorities of crime prevention. This may be especially true in small island jurisdictions where supplying the foundation infrastructure of a criminal justice system can be expected to take a larger than proportional amount from public coffers. Supplying the foundations or fixed-cost items may severely limit the real capacity of the system by restricting the ability to pay for the variable inputs required for actual operation.

In small island economies with severe constraints on their law enforcement capabilities, one might expect policy makers to follow the lead of wealthier societies and minimize attention given to victimless crimes. In the United States the laws against some such crimes have been eased (Hellman, 1980, 133). Hellman points out that public drunkenness has been decriminalized in many states and alludes to diminished penalties for marijuana use, coupled with a low priority being given to arrests for the use of that drug (1980, 133). He refers to "adult entertainment centers, which in effect legalize prostitution within their boundaries, [which] have been proposed in some major cities" and goes on to mention state-run lotteries (Hellman, 1980, 133).

The arguments for decriminalizing activities such as those cited above are familiar. Without attempting to resolve the controversies surrounding such proposals, suffice it to say that their very existence may support a low priority for victimless crimes in Third World nations in general and more particularly in the small island jurisdictions under discussion. By ignoring such activities smaller and poorer nations would presumably free public funds for use in "more crucial" crime prevention programs, not to mention other projects of concern.

In some cases activities regarded as criminal in most developed nations may appear to be making positive contributions to Third World economies. The most obvious current examples of this phenomenon are drug related. The involvement of the rural underclasses of Third World nations in growing drug crops and processing and shipping drugs has been widespread and appears to be growing with the rising international market for recreational drugs. The seeming permanence and stability of that market is seductive when compared to the well-known vagaries of world markets for various other staple commodities.

In economies where other export crops are in trouble and where employment options are minimal, public officials' placing a low priority on eradicating an export-oriented drug industry is hardly surprising. Besides providing employment opportunities and needed hard currency balances, it may slow the tide of urban migration and, as a result, the incidence of various crimes related to the necessities of survival in an urban underclass. That governments in the Andean region of Latin America, not to mention Central America and the Caribbean, may share an ambivalence against foreign pressure to eradicate drug crops, much less processing facilities and export networks, should not be too surprising.

The positive effects of the industry may seem obvious and perhaps superior to less obvious negative influences. The employment the industry provides and its ability to bring in needed foreign exchange may prove persuasive for governments considered honest. As long as the products of the industry are largely exported, the industry itself, if considered criminal at all, may be cast in the category of victimless crime. In a domestic sense this may be accurate, at least initially. Thus the drug trade may receive low priority in terms of public willingness to commit law enforcement resources to its control.

In the Caribbean Basin, Jamaica may be an example of this phenomenon. Marijuana, known locally as ganja, is a fairly common drug among poor Jamaicans. Indeed certain religious groups make ritualistic use of the herb (Owens, 1976; Nicholas, 1979). In a nation that has been close to bankruptcy during the 1980s, marijuana has proven to be a reliable cash crop for export. Although not a legal industry, the utility of marijuana export was certainly recognized by the government, as evidenced by the easing of deposit controls imposed upon commercial banks in order to facilitate the movement of U.S. currency within the economy. Because the currency in question undoubtedly originated in the ganja trade, the pragmatism of the rather conservative Seaga regime was recognizable. Jamaica and various other Caribbean economies are well positioned to compete effectively in the North American market for marijuana.

A recent study of coca and cocaine production in Peru shows that negative impacts are also possible from the production of drugs for export (Morales, 1986, 143–161). Not the least of such negative impacts is the "increasing dependency of the peasantry and the unemployed on the underground cocaine world" (Morales, 1986, 144). Growing cash drug crops for export, while perhaps providing various short-run benefits, locks those involved even at the most menial level into permanent association with the international drug industry. Tastes acquired and satisfied through drug-related employment are not as easily serviced in alternative pursuits (Morales, 1986).

Aside from growing marijuana, various small island economies of the Caribbean Basin region have become involved in the transshipment of that commodity and other drugs, notably cocaine. Perhaps the most notable example of that activity has been occurring in the Bahamas. That nation, with its innumerable islands, many of which are relatively remote, lends itself well to the transshipment of contraband into southern Florida. With its population concentrated on a relatively small number of islands, the priorities of domestic law enforcement hardly dictate dispatching substantial security forces to police the more remote regions of the country.

If the residents of those remote Bahamian islands gain temporary employment in transshipment activities, the immediate net effect might be positive. Unfortunately, the real cost benefit balance began shifting toward the negative with the increasing involvement of Bahamians in the drug culture and a resultant increase in other forms of criminal activity, particularly crimes of violence. In a nation known for low rates of violent crime (de Albuquerque, 1984, 116) this development emphasizes the risks inherent in any form of involvement in the drug trade and, of course, speaks to the need for priority status for such activities on the rolls of local law enforcement agencies.

Although the involvement of small island states in the drug trade and other illegal activities may increase their national incomes, this extra income may be very unevenly distributed. For example, growers of marijuana, because of competition and low risk of prosecution, may obtain a return not significantly higher than that from the alternative most profitable use of their land whereas dealers in drugs, especially organizers of the international trade, can be expected to take the lion's share of rents. Organizers of the drug trade and of prostitution catering to tourists in developing countries are often foreigners.

Those involved in criminal economic activity often fail to pay their taxes. Nevertheless, criminals make use of infrastructure provided by the state, and their activities can lead to an increase in secondary crime, e.g., theft by drug users, which necessitates greater expenditure on law enforcement.

The location of criminal activities is affected by economic factors, such as the proximity of the country to markets, the size of markets, and the extent of competition from other countries. The Caribbean islands are well placed in relation to the U.S. market but face competition from Latin American countries. Latin American countries are strong competitors in the production and distribution of drugs. But in relation to criminal activities that thrive on international tourism, such as prostitution, the Latin American countries, with the possible exception of Mexico, would not seem to be strong competitors for U.S. tourist dollars.

In comparison, the South Pacific islands have much smaller markets for the sale of illegal goods and services, being principally dependent on the Australian and New Zealand market. It is widely believed that Papua New Guinea acts as a channel for distribution of drugs to Australia because of its proximity to northern Australia, which is remote and sparsely populated. Light aircraft are reputed to carry drugs from Papua New

Guinea at night and land on airstrips at remote cattle stations (ranches) or on landing strips constructed during World War II. Sailing boats plying around the Pacific from Indonesia and Papua New Guinea also appear to facilitate the drug trade.

As for the growing and production of drugs, South Pacific countries face considerable competition from Southeast Asian countries, such as Thailand and the Philippines. In the supply of illegal goods and services, such as prostitution and drugs to international travelers, the Pacific islands seem to have an economic disadvantage compared to Bali, the Philippines, and Thailand. It is not much more expensive for Australians to visit most Southeast Asian countries than most Pacific islands, and Southeast Asian countries seem to offer a greater range of tourist attractions. Thus international criminal activity in the small island states of the South Pacific appears to be on a smaller scale than in the Caribbean.

Nevertheless, the above should not be taken to indicate that drug problems in the South Pacific islands are minimal. Drug trafficking is reported to be increasing. It has been claimed that cannabis (marijuana) grown in the Papua New Guinea Highlands is of good quality and cheaper than that from many other sources and that corrupt politicians may be involved with gangs in the trafficking (*Pacific Islands Monthly,* May 1988, 28). With falling coffee prices and threats to coffee crops from a recently introduced rust, cannabis may be a tempting alternative cash crop for some coffee growers (De Silva and Tisdell, 1988). Australian crime authorities visiting Fiji recently stated that the Pacific states increasingly are being used to reroute drugs, particularly cocaine as the U.S. market becomes saturated (*Pacific Islands Monthly,* May 1, 1988, 40). Offshore banking systems in the Pacific islands are also being used to "launder" drug money.

A special drug exported from the Pacific is kava, a drink made from the roots of the kava plant. The long-term health effects of taking the drug are unknown. For a time the United States Food and Drug Administration banned the import of kava powder to the United States, but the ban was dropped in 1986. Recently, the Vanuatu government has decided to encourage the export of the drug to assist its economy.

Another form of crime, which may be viewed as victimless in the domestic sense, encompasses various forms of international financial manipulation. This category of activity may include parking funds, money laundering, tax evasion, capital flight, and securities, investment, and real estate fraud. The successful harboring of such activities presupposes state-of-the-art transportation and communications linkages, political stability, and, of course, a sound financial system committed to bank secrecy.

Arguments presented elsewhere raise doubts concerning the general viability of offshore banking as a vehicle for development (McKee, 1988, 77–84). Despite the existence of some notably successful Third World offshore banking centers, the new locations "most willing to enter the field are often among the smallest and weakest in the Third World" (McKee, 1988, 83). If such locations are hoping to use offshore banking as one of the underpinnings for a development strategy, they must consider the nature of their potential clientele. Given the array of successful offshore centers already available, who will the new centers be able to attract as customers, assuming that they can attract banks to service them?

It is quite possible that a decision to elect such a development strategy may implicitly select some of the questionable financial activities alluded to earlier. Among the lists of potential customers for newer, perhaps less competitive offshore centers, may be included drug traffickers, gun runners, and persons engaged in various forms of organized and nonorganized criminal activities (Walter, 1985, 3). Banks in the new centers may have to accept such clients to ensure a critical mass of business, or they may have established themselves fully intending to court such a customer base.

Conceivably, those in charge of selecting development options in smaller, weaker island economies may view questionable international financial transactions as victimless crimes with respect to the domestic economy. In cases where such impressions prevail and are translated into policy, doors are being opened to admit permanent linkages between the small economies in question and the international criminal underworld.

Writing in 1985, Ingo Walter cited various reasons for the Caribbean region's becoming "abundantly supplied with secrecy havens" (Walter, 1985, 108). Among reasons cited were ease of communications and closeness to the United States and the consequent constraints on political risks. He also suggested that "location is important for attracting Latin American flight capital" and that the Region's "positioning astride one of the world's major drug routes" contributes as well (Walter, 1988, 108).

For these reasons, coupled with the realities of smallness and rather limited growth options, Walter suggested that the "financial secrecy business has a great deal to recommend it to planners seeking economic progress" (Walter, 1985, 108). On the surface at least, the encouragement of offshore banking among the small island economies of the Caribbean region would appear to supply substantial employment opportunities, not to mention often scarce foreign currency balances. Based upon their perceptions, the industry may appear to harbor great potential as a growth stimulant. The presumed successes of existing offshore centers provide a powerful, ongoing demonstration effect. Thus, various Caribbean jurisdictions are encouraging the industry. Aside from established offshore centers like the Bahamas, the Cayman Islands, and locations in the Netherlands Antilles, various other Caribbean economies are encouraging similar development.

The same is true in the Pacific. Such financial centers exist in Tonga, Vanuatu, Cook Islands, Nauru, and the Marshall Islands. Kiribati is considering developing one. All protect offshore account holders with punitive secrecy provisions, and all are susceptible to criminal activity (*Pacific Islands Monthly,* April/May 1989, 31). Despite this, most of these economies see the centers as a source of some employment. For example, the center in Vanuatu is said to employ 400 people, a small number but useful when so few employment opportunities exist (*Pacific Islands Monthly,* April/May 1989, 31). Fraud involving establishing banks (shell banks) without adequate funds is increasing in the islands, and the *Pacific Islands Monthly* (April/May 1989, 31) states: "Even the Marshall Islands is in on the act, and while it is difficult to estimate the result of issuing banking licenses in terms of the country's financial reputation, the long-term effect cannot be favorable."

Much evidence exists concerning illegal activity in existing offshore centers. Using U.S. government data sources, Ingo Walter has compiled a litany of cases involving offshore banking centers (Walter, 1985, 195–203). The Cayman Islands were cited in 11 cases involving money laundering or the illegal secretion of profits. The Bahamas were involved in seven. In the case of the Cayman Islands, offenses included laundering kickbacks, and drug profits, secreting profits from pornography, embezzled funds, and kickbacks. In the Bahamas embezzled funds and kickbacks were laundered, together with the profits from prostitution and drugs, and the profits from securities fraud were secreted. Two cases involving the Netherlands Antilles included laundering drug profits and secreting divested corporate funds.

The Walter litany continues with cases involving the "secreting of legitimate assets for illegitimate purposes" (Walter, 1985, 197). In issues of this sort, the Cayman islands were cited in six cases as compared to three for the Bahamas. Offenses in the Caymans included four instances of secreting funds to evade taxes, diverting corporate receipts, and secreting funds to be used in kickbacks. In the Bahamas two cases involved secreting corporate funds for illegal campaign contributions, and the third involved tax evasion.

No fewer than nine Caribbean economies were listed as having been used as integral parts of overall criminal schemes (Walter, 1985, 198–202). The Bahamas were cited 15 times. Specific schemes included the use of banks to honor and/or promote worthless checks, the use of banks, trusts, and corporations for securities fraud, and the use of corporations to set up fraudulent tax shelters to defraud. Included among other activities were placing security funds in foreign accounts for purposes of tax evasion, aiding in false representation to the IRS with respect to activities in foreign countries, as well as taking false deductions involving foreign corporations, not to mention secreting property.

Among 11 cases involving the Cayman islands, 4 involved using foreign banks and/or corporations to establish fraudulent tax shelters. Other tax-related cases involved using foreign accounts to defraud and evade taxes and taking false deductions involving foreign tax shelters and/or corporations. Foreign corporations and subsidiaries were used to bribe foreign officials, to commit securities fraud, and to violate securities regulations. Another violation involved deducting costs that were eventually returned through foreign accounts.

Although the Bahamas and the Cayman islands housed the bulk of the offenders, similar cases occurred in various other Caribbean locations. Sham double trusts were uncovered in the Turks and Caicos Islands and Belize. The Turks and Caicos were also the site of a case involving the use of foreign accounts to commit exchange fraud. Cases of fraud, tax evasion, and other violations occurred in Anguilla, Antigua, Montserrat, and St. Vincent, as well as Puerto Rico, despite that island's ties to the United States.

Many Australian companies appear to use tax havens in the Pacific to minimize Australian tax payments. Trading companies can transfer profit offshore by reinvoicing. For example, goods to be shipped from Japan to Australia may be invoiced to a company in the Cook Islands, which in turn charges its associated company in Australia an inflated price. Or the company in the tax haven may charge its associated Australian company an inflated price for whatever service it provides for the Australian company. The Australian government is planning to introduce new laws to deal with the problem (*Pacific Islands Monthly*, April/May 1989, 31).

The activities cited above deserve the attention of those concerned with developmental issues in small island economies. From various forms of involvement in the drug trade, to international financial machinations of a questionable nature, they may appear to be relatively victimless in a domestic sense. This feature may ensure that they are given rather low priority in the pecking order of tasks to be financed through public funds. The probability that they may actually provide a certain amount of employment may ensure them of even less public concern. When the fact that they may earn needed foreign exchange is added to the mix, they may be dropped from the pecking order of problems altogether or even quietly supported by governments not otherwise given to moral laxities.

The main point to be recognized seems to be that small island economies may be particularly susceptible to the types of activities discussed above. Such pursuits may permanently involve the nations in question in international criminal activities. Such involvements may lead to the corruption of public officials and the increase of domestic criminal activity. In the case of drugs, the involvement of local residents in actual drug use may lead to an increase of crime against persons and property. Such developments in small economies may be sufficient to preclude more mainstream forms of material advancement and, thus, may alter development options irreparably.

Another subset of criminal activity that may impact the development prospects of small island jurisdictions is composed of offenses against tourists and foreign nationals. "High tourist densities generate increased hostility on the part of the host population towards tourists, and this hostility often manifests itself in increased criminal activity against both tourist and local populations" (de Albuquerque, 1984, 113). In this context de Albuquerque was presumably referring to violent and perhaps even irrational attacks upon tourists.

Although incidents of this sort can and do occur in SINs, they are probably not representative of the bulk of offenses committed against foreigners. Speaking of the Caribbean area, de Albuquerque found, "The relationship between tourist arrivals and murder/manslaughter is positive but not statistically significant" (de Albuquerque, 1984, 119). Probably offenses against foreigners, like crime in general, have a more rational motivation.

Violent crimes even though committed rationally for gain cannot help hurting tourism. Even property crimes of a nonviolent nature can give tourist destinations an unsavory reputation. Wherever relatively affluent visitors congregate in Third World settings, a certain amount of crime directed toward them is inevitable. A certain amount may have to be written off the priority lists of those concerned with law enforcement. However, when the purse snatchers, pickpockets, smash and grab artists, and petty con merchants reach a noticeable mass, the result will be adverse publicity and, in extreme cases, tourist advisories. Vacationers will be unlikely to continue frequenting destinations where such offenses surmount what they have been used to at home.

In Papua New Guinea, murder, rape, robbery, and violence generally have become a serious problem, and many of these crimes are committed against foreigners. The incidence of these crimes deters both foreign investment and personnel from working in the country and keeps foreign tourists from visiting. In recent times, for example, the United States Department of State has warned U.S. citizens that there is a continuing crime problem both in rural and urban areas and that they should not travel alone. This year the huge Bougainville copper mine in Papua New Guinea was forced to close because of violence by a local group attempting "to extort" money from the operators. In relation to tourists, the Minister of Culture and Tourism in Papua New Guinea has expressed concern, pointing out that tourism will definitely be affected by widespread crime in Papua New Guinea (*Pacific Islands Monthly,* May 1988).

Small island economies that have opted to emphasize tourism in their development plans will have a vested interest in ensuring that their visitor accommodations, beaches, golf courses, and other facilities are reasonably safe. Another aspect of relatively petty crime directed at visitors is its ability to grow or spread. Tastes generated through successful petty criminal activities may grow and possibly require more serious offenses to be satisfied. In various Caribbean destinations where tourism is seasonal, the off-season may see an increase in criminal offenses aimed at the local population. Small island jurisdictions involved in tourism may have a vested interest in suppressing even nonviolent and, perhaps, petty offenses aimed at visitors.

The debate over victimless crime in SINs must also consider the role played by such activities with respect to visitors. Destinations that elect to "service" the needs of visitors, irrespective of the nature of those needs, will over time determine the nature of the visitors themselves and, hence, the nature of the tourist industry. Tours designed to satisfy various basic appetites have been well known in certain Third World destinations (O'Grady, 1982, 35–41). SINs electing to encourage such traffic may generate irreversible social and economic impacts.

Tourism generates a certain amount of victimless crime. The most militantly moralistic enforcement regime probably could not completely expunge certain sexual favors from the list of commercial services available to visitors. However, such a regime might conceivably curtail some of the more undesirable excesses. Barring extreme measures against both purveyors and users, it is also doubtful that SINs could completely interdict the use of recreational drugs among visiting tourists.

In a practical vein, stopping activities such as those mentioned above may not be possible in SINs, where tourism has a central economic role. That being the case, the reasonable fallback position may be one involving an attempt to minimize the adverse impact of such activities upon the host jurisdiction. In the case of recreational drugs, the risks appear to be threefold. First is the risk referred to in the earlier discussion of drugs, involving elements of the local population in permanent, international criminal networks. Second, there is the risk of increasing drug use among the local population due to such substances being more readily available. Finally, there is the risk of increases in other forms of criminal activity as users require more and more funds to supply their needs.

In small island settings, the risks inherent in offering commercialized sexual favors for tourists have generally been noneconomic, unless one considers the opportunity costs of those involved in such pursuits. In recent years the advent of AIDS and, to a lesser extent, certain other sexually communicated diseases has introduced serious cost considerations.

Certain areas in the Caribbean are already feeling the impact of AIDS. Haiti is the nation most often referred to in this regard. There is little doubt that male prostitution has contributed to the impact of the malady in that setting. In Caribbean resort areas, male prostitutes service clients of both genders. Thus, visitors are at risk, but so are local sexually active populations. The economic risks come from at least two directions. First, the fear of AIDS could reduce visitors, resulting in excess capacity and financial losses for the tourist industry. Second, the spread of AIDS among island populations could result in a serious burden on existing medical resources, not to mention a forced reordering of public priorities, which could very well harm development-related projects.

While AIDS is not yet as serious a problem in the Pacific islands as in the Caribbean, it is on the increase. But as yet, tourism is not believed to be an important source of transmission of the AIDS virus in the Pacific islands (South Pacific Commission, 1988, 9). Constraints on sexual education and aversion to the use of condoms by some island groups could add to difficulties controlling the spread of the disease in the islands (*Pacific Islands Monthly*, February 1989, 10).

In the new health climate surrounding commercialized sex in SINs, public priorities may require some reordering. The provision of safe commercial experiences and, hence, some assurance against major domestic difficulties may be well beyond both the willingness and the resources of the jurisdictions in question. If that is the case, steps may be required to discourage the industry. Domestically that may require heavier law enforcement expenditures. It may also require additional advertising expenditures designed to attract visitors with less risky recreational preferences.

All things considered, it seems certain crimes considered victimless in some nations may well require public attention in small island economies because of their potential for negative impacts. Also, certain activities that may not be considered crimes domestically but that lock certain elements of the population into ongoing international criminal liaisons should also be high on the priority lists of public officials. Because of the potential impact of the practices discussed in this chapter, they should be outranked in public priority pecking orders only by violent activities, which head such lists in most of the world's nations.

Criminal activities and liaisons by political and public leaders in small island states are all too common (Crocombe, 1989, 5). As Crocombe (1989, 6) points out, "There are cases already known in several Pacific countries of international crime figures having close personal links with island political leaders. The small size and small economies make leaders especially vulnerable."

III

Environmental and Natural Resource Issues

10

Agriculture in the Developmental Mix

This chapter concentrates on the importance of agriculture as an economic activity in island microstates and considers economic problems faced by their agricultural sectors. But at the outset it should be noted that the degree of dependence of island economies on agriculture varies considerably. A few are more dependent upon fishing than agriculture. In some exceptional cases, mineral exports are more important than agricultural exports, and in at least one case in the South Pacific exports of forest products are of greater value than agricultural exports. However, in virtually all cases, underdeveloped island microstates are heavily dependent upon economic production directly related to using or exploiting natural resources. This is true of agriculture, fishing, forestry, and mining.

Certain problems related to staple production were discussed earlier in the present volume (Chapter 1). As for agriculture, its success depends, among other things, on the availability of suitable land and climate. Some island countries consisting of coral atolls, e.g., Tuvalu, the Maldives, and Kiribati, have little land mass, and their soil is of poor quality for agriculture. Islands in these archipelagoes are limey coral outcrops with soils lacking humus and having little ability to retain moisture. The inhabitants of such countries tend to be more dependent on marine resources than on agriculture for their livelihood in contrast to island countries principally of volcanic origin, e.g., Fiji, Samoa, parts of Papua New Guinea, and the Solomon Islands, or those islands mainly of continental origin, e.g., New Caledonia. The differences will become clear if we consider some economic statistics for seven South Pacific island states recently reviewed by the International Monetary Fund (Browne and Scott, 1989). The countries are Fiji, Kiribati, Papua New Guinea, Solomon Islands, Samoa, Tonga, and Vanuatu.

In the case of Fiji, sugar and molasses (obtained from cane sugar) accounted for 58.9% of the value of its exports in 1987. This together

· with gold, fish, forest products, and coconut oil (which is of relatively minor value) accounted for 87% of the value of Fiji's exports in 1987. Statistics on the relative importance of agriculture in the Fijian economy are limited, but in 1987 agriculture, forestry, and fishing accounted for 24.5% of GDP at factor cost.

In contrast fishing was much more important in relation to the economy of Kiribati, an atoll economy. Fishing products, including shark fins, accounted for 78% of the value of the exports of Kiribati, and copra, 20% in 1986. Together these items constituted 98% of the value of Kiribati's exports in 1986. Other statistics also confirm the major economic role of fishing in Kiribati, which is comprised of coral atolls. Whereas agriculture accounted for 12.75% of GDP in Kiribati in 1986, fisheries made a 16.42% contribution to GDP.

Papua New Guinea is a relatively large country, and one can legitimately raise some doubt about whether it should be included among small island states. Being a relatively large country, it has a more diversified export portfolio than many microstates. However, it is heavily dependent, as are most developing microstates, on exports of primary products. Papua New Guinea has become heavily dependent on mineral exports for foreign exchange earnings. In 1987, gold was its most valuable export followed by copper. Together gold, copper, and silver accounted for 62.4% of the value of Papua New Guinea's exports. Coffee, cocoa, palm oil, copra, and coconut oil (in decreasing value) accounted for about 22% of the value of its exports. But the importance of agriculture to Papua New Guinea's economy for employment and regional development is much greater than these figures may indicate.

While agriculture contributed 35.9% of the GDP of the Solomon Islands in 1987, it was less important as an export earner. It contributed 20.96% of the value of exports, the value of these exports being less than for fish, logs, and sawn timber. The main agricultural commodities entering international trade were copra, palm oil, and cocoa. In this economy, the contribution to GDP of nonmonetary or subsistence agriculture is approximately equal to that of commercial (monetary) agriculture. Subsistence agriculture is still very important in many islands of the Pacific, and in many it employs the majority of rural people.

Agriculture is relatively important in Tonga. In 1987–1988, it accounted for 33.28% of GDP at factor price. Forestry, mining, and quarrying were of negligible significance. Also agriculture accounted for most of Tonga's exports, but fish exports were of some significance. In 1987–1988, Tonga's main exports in decreasing value were coconut derived products, fish, vanilla beans, bananas, and root crops. In 1987,

Vanuatu's main exports by value were (in decreasing order) copra, beef, cocoa, cut logs, and sawn timber. Together these natural-resource intensive items accounted for 78.35% of the value of Vanuatu's exports in 1987. In 1987, Western Samoa mainly relied on agricultural produce for export income but also earned a small amount from timber exports.

It can be seen that in common with most developing island states, Pacific island countries and many in the Caribbean rely heavily on primary exports for export income. Furthermore a few (limited range of) commodities account for the bulk of their export income. Their exports are not diversified, and this exposes them to price fluctuations and other risks in the commodities they export. Historically, primary commodities have shown considerable price fluctuation, and a number of countries in the Pacific have set up commodity price stabilization funds in an attempt to moderate fluctuations in the price paid to agricultural producers for their export produce.

Given the nature and limited range of their exports, developing island countries face considerable risks in engaging in international trade and specializing in production to satisfy this trade. Not only do they expose themselves to fluctuating prices of primary commodities, but also occasionally the demand for a commodity in which they have specialized can collapse completely or almost so because of the development of substitutes, e.g., artificial vanilla as a replacement for natural vanilla. On the production side, natural disasters such as hurricanes or cyclones can severely affect available supplies of agricultural produce for export, and many island states are in areas subject to such disasters.

Few Caribbean economies can boast of avoiding the wrath of hurricanes. Those weather systems have been widely cited in a causal role vis-à-vis agricultural difficulties. In 1988 and 1989 Jamaica and Puerto Rico, together with various smaller islands, were severely damaged by tropical weather systems.

Also the agricultural supplies may be at risk from accidentally introduced pests and diseases. For example, the occurrence of yellowing disease in coconuts almost eliminated the varieties of coconut originally grown in the Caribbean, and accidentally introduced coffee rust poses a threat to the coffee crop in Papua New Guinea (De Silva and Tisdell, 1988).

In many of the Pacific islands a considerable amount of agriculture and fishing is of a subsistence type. We have already noted this in the case of the Solomon Islands. Plantations exist in the South Pacific, but they do not account for more than half of commercial production of most agricultural crops, unlike in the Caribbean. In commercial agriculture, small holdings are a relatively important source of supply in the Pacific islands compared to the Caribbean. Thus, in contrast to the Caribbean, subsistence agriculture and small commercial holdings are common in the Pacific.

There has been much debate about the wisdom of Pacific islanders abandoning subsistence agriculture for commercial agriculture. Although neoclassical economic theory stresses the advantages of markets and of specialization in trade, according to comparative advantage, such specialization can have adverse side effects. It can mean greater exposure to risk as mentioned above. It may lock island countries into dependence on center countries. For example, having specialized in particular commodities, island countries may try to negotiate special contracts with larger importers. Mauritius has done this with the European Economic Community (EEC) and the United States for sugar, and so has Fiji. In turn this may reduce somewhat the political independence of island countries.

Commercialization can also be expected to hasten the breakdown of traditional social structures. Unlike in the Caribbean, the Pacific islands are still in the main inhabited by their indigenous people. The main exception is Fiji, where East Indians account for about half the population. They were originally brought in by the British to work as indentured laborers on sugar cane plantations. Hawaii is another exception, and there are also a large number of French settlers in New Caledonia. Traditional societies in the Pacific islands are organized on a communal ownership basis involving sharing arrangements under the direction of a village chief or chiefs. In contrast the market system tends to emphasize the motive of individual self-interest and the benefits of private property compared to communal property. Under the influence of the market system, traditional societies tend to disintegrate. Whether one judges this to be a good or bad thing depends upon one's evaluation of traditional societies compared to market system economies in which self-interest, resource mobility, and private property tend to prevail. On the whole policy makers in island countries appear to have favored commercialization, but this may be a reflection of urban bias (Lipton, 1975; 1977). In contrast a number of academics have not been convinced about the social virtues of whole-hearted commercialization for these small island states (Bertram, 1986; Connell, 1988; Tisdell and Fairbairn, 1984; Fairbairn, 1985).

According to Connell (1988, 37) subsistence agriculture has universally declined in island microstates. Dependence on foreign food or "dietary colonialism" is claimed to have increased, and, with the decline in subsistence agriculture, the variety of planted species has declined, making agriculture more vulnerable to natural hazards and to fluctuations in world commodity prices. Furthermore, "the simultaneous decline in subsistence agricultural production and growing consumption of imported food (especially tinned meat and fish, rice biscuits and flour) both by reducing the regularity of food consumption (as cash flows are variable) and increasing the consumption of sugar, especially has substantially increased the incidence of diet related diseases such as diabetes" (Connell, 1988, 37).

In the Caribbean "people suffer from an increasing problem of nutritional deficiency because of the region's inability to feed itself" (Barry et al., 1984, 29). The same authors go on to suggest that more than 50% of the population is deficient in protein and calories (quoting Delimore, 1979, 56). "Nutrition-linked ills include energy and protein deficiency, iron-deficiency anemia, obesity, and related health problems like hypertension and diabetes" (Barry et al., 1984, 29).

In the region "the total domination by export crop production of cultivable land set the stage for . . . inadequate food production" (Barry et al., 1984, 28–29). Using history as a reminder, it has been suggested that the "reliance on imported food brought disaster when the North American Revolution and birth of the United States interrupted supplies" (Barry et al., 1984, 29). Barry and his colleagues went on to say, "Between 1780 and 1787, more than 15,000 plantation workers in Jamaica died of famine." Those authors are of the opinion that the wide availability of imported foods has hurt the attainment of self-sufficiency in basic food production (Barry et al., 1984, 29). Whether complete self-sufficiency is a necessary goal remains to be seen. Reducing food imports not only puts people to work, thus generating income, it also reduces an unnecessary drain on needed foreign exchange.

In specializing in the export of agricultural and natural resource-based commodities, island economies face another difficulty, namely the long-term tendency for the terms of trade to turn against such commodities, as for example noted by Prebisch (1950) and others (Singer, 1950; Gillis et al., 1983, Ch. 15). This has resulted in calls for SINs to specialize to a greater extent in the production of manufacturing goods and in tertiary industries (Connell, 1988, 42). However, in manufacturing industries most SINs are at a comparative economic disadvantage. They lack large home markets and so have difficulties in obtaining scale economies. Many are remote from large international markets and considerable transport and communication costs may need to be incurred by them to market their products. In addition, they often lack a skilled labor force, some (atoll islands in particular) lack water supplies essential for some types of manufacture, and many are deficient in energy resources. This is not to deny that island states can be successful in manufacturing. Hong Kong and Singapore provide examples. But among other things these islands have some location advantages compared, for instance, to South Pacific island states.

Why has the relative economic importance of subsistence agriculture and agriculture in general tended to decline in island nations? In the Pacific, Bertram (1986) and Bertram and Watters (1985; 1986) have attributed this largely to the dependence of these countries on foreign aid and remittances coupled with international migration possibilities for the inhabitants of some of these nations. Foreign exchange inflows from aid and remittances have tended to cause the currencies of island nations to appreciate, thus making their commodities, including agricultural produce, more expensive in terms of foreign currency. But more important, foreign aid expenditures have tended to be concentrated in urban areas and have been used to expand government employment, thus providing an incentive for individuals to leave agriculture. Remittances from relatives living abroad (or in local urban areas) mean that recipients are not so dependent on agriculture (if they are agriculturalists) to earn a living and can either shift out of it or reduce their effort or productivity. Furthermore, in cases where there are opportunities to migrate abroad, often the younger men migrate. Because this group may make a higher than average contribution to agricultural output in their home country, a loss in agricultural production can be expected. This group is also most likely to migrate first to urban areas in their own country, and this internal migration will have a similar effect.

Foreign aid inflows and remittances tend to lead to economic restructuring of these economies. Their impact has been likened to that of the Dutch disease (see Gillis et al., 1983, 438, 528–55) whereby a sudden increase in the demand for an export commodity, the production of which may not be very labor intensive, such as oil, leads to appreciation of a country's currency and the decline of its traditional industries. The industries that decline, however, may be those that would be most sustainable in the long run. Some writers believe that a Dutch-type economic disease is leading to the decline of agriculture in many SINs and that this has been brought on by foreign aid inflows and remittances.

Although foreign capital inflows and remittances have contributed to the decline of the agricultural sector in many SINs, other factors may also have played a role. With the passage of time, opportunities for expansion of industries in the secondary and tertiary sectors have increased. At least in the larger microstates, a relative decline in the agricultural sector could have been expected on that basis in any case. This restructuring is also reinforced by demand-pull factors in those countries in which per capita incomes have risen. This is because the demand for agricultural produce is relatively income inelastic. Furthermore, with increased education, better educated youths have become less willing to adopt agriculture as a vocation.

In the Caribbean region there is an aversion to agricultural labor in some circles (Beckford, 1972; 1983). Because field work was initially the preserve of slaves and later of indentured labor, even today it is frowned upon in many areas. The result is underproduction and, in many cases, the excessive import of food. In St. Vincent and the Grenadines, "substantial quantities of livestock and fishery products imported could be produced locally" (World Bank, 1985f, 14). In Dominica, "measures required to bring idle and underutilized land into full production [and] to increase agricultural productivity are underway" (World Bank, 1985b, 11).

In St. Christopher and Nevis, "potential exists for a wide range of vegetable and fruit crops, including tomatoes, carrots, cabbages, egg-plants and citrus" as well as for increasing domestic livestock production (World Bank, 1985d, 12). In Grenada, "the newly elected government has made the revitalization of agriculture the keystone of the efforts to promote economic growth" (World Bank, 1985c, 8).

Although governmental agencies in the region appear to have some interest in the problems of agriculture, that interest does not always include the production of foodstuffs for domestic consumption. In general, as emphasized earlier (Chapter 1), in relation to international trade, the long-run terms of trade have moved against agriculture. This can also be expected to lead to a decline in employment in agriculture even though a "perverse" response is possible, that is, a response in which farmers try to increase production to compensate for reduced income.

In the last respect, reactions of subsistence/small landholders may be different from those on plantations. Decisions on plantations are likely to be guided principally by the profit motive whereas there is evidence, for example, from small coffee holdings in the Highlands of Papua New Guinea that their cultivators are guided by the desire to earn with minimum effort a target level of cash income (De Silva and Tisdell, 1988). Consequently, whereas falling prices or rising costs are likely to cause plantations (profit-maximizers) to reduce production, these are likely to result in greater production by small landholders (satificers) as they increase their effort to attain their cash income targets.

In most developing island states, agricultural productivity is below potential (Browne and Scott, 1989, 7). As pointed out by the Australian Centre for International Agricultural Research (ACIAR), some policy advisors suggest that agriculture in the South Pacific should provide more food for increasing populations, provide substitutes for imported food, earn foreign exchange, provide more cash for farmers, and generate employment. Even though there is scope to increase levels of agricultural production, especially in the subsistence sector, so far agricultural development has been disappointing. ACIAR states that "productivity has been low; cash incomes have not increased; export volumes have not expanded rapidly; and increased employment opportunities have not matched population increases. Various biological, social, economic and political factors have been cited as limiting increased agricultural production" (quoted by Joint Committee on Foreign Affairs, Defence and Trade, 1989, 17).

Speaking of the need to reduce food imports in the Caribbean region, William Demas suggested, "What is involved . . . is not only import *substitution* (for example, growing strawberries or grapes at home instead of importing them)" (1988a, 163). Demas went on to say that the real need is for "import replacement — that is the use of products indigenous to the Region to replace imported products which cannot be grown at home" (1988a, 163). He cites an example of a producer in Guyana (often considered to be a Caribbean nation) who is planning to manufacture cereals and snacks from "flours derived from casava, rice and plantain" (Demas, 1988a, 163).

In spite of the obvious logic in what Demas has suggested, barriers hinder moving in the direction he recommended. Discussing obstacles facing an agriculture oriented toward domestic markets in the Caribbean, Jean Crusol cited various issues (1980, 122). Among them was the traditional indifference of officialdom. In addition he referred to the power and lack of flexibility in large plantations as well as the dependent relationship existing between small farms and large estates. Other problems cited included a taste for imports and the external slant of island business (Crusol, 1980, 122 ff.).

Although Crusol was correct in citing official indifference toward producing for domestic markets, that problem is not universal throughout the region. In the Bahamas, for example, "The Government attaches considerable policy importance to the expansion of domestic agricultural production to reduce import dependence" (World Bank, 1986, 31). By and large that nation has never been very successful in large-scale export-oriented agricultural operations. Unlike many other Caribbean jurisdictions, its soil and topography made it only marginally attractive as a location for plantation crops. In the mid 1980s agriculture in the Bahamas was "dominated by small scale operations with production of poultry, fruit and vegetables for the local market, with some exports of citrus fruit and seasonal vegetables" (World Bank, 1986, 15). According to the World Bank, roughly 85% of consumed food is imported (1986, 31).

Although agricultural production in Antigua and Barbuda has been moving away "from plantation crops, such as cotton and sugar, towards a more diversified system of fruits and vegetables," the sector "has been in a steady decline since the mid-1970's, and despite a variety of efforts, the performance of the sector is considerably below potential" (World Bank, 1986, 15). Despite the unused potential, the World Bank saw the "sector's ability to generate substantial employment opportunities in the near to medium term" as doubtful and recommended tourism, manufacturing, and trade as offering greater scope for growth and employment (World Bank, 1986, 16). No doubt the same prognosis might apply to the Bahamas.

In Barbados, "The share of agriculture and fishing in GDP has declined significantly since the 1950's when it contributed over 30%" (World Bank, 1988, 11). According to the report cited, agriculture and fishing have fallen to a 9% to 10% share of GDP in recent years, with the decline attributed to the fading fortunes of sugar (1988, 11–12).

When productivity per unit area is taken as the index, productivity is lower for commercial crops on most small holdings than on plantations. This, for example, is the case for coffee production in Papua New Guinea. Plantations tend to make greater use of modern techniques and purchased inputs, such as fertilizers and pesticides and appear to be better managed or managed with a different objective in mind compared to many small holdings.

Browne and Scott (1989, 8) suggest that shortages of trained managers in the South Pacific islands have limited expansion in commercial agriculture since the independence era. They go on to point out that production in the plantation sector has stagnated or declined in Papua New Guinea with the exit of expatriate managers. In Western Samoa, the establishment of public sector estates is claimed to have inhibited agricultural revitalization. Although in the Solomon Islands, the establishment of plantation joint ventures between the government and foreign private investors, such as Unilever, resulted in production gains in the commercial sector, this thrust has not been sustained. Browne and Scott (1989, 8) argue that difficulties in increasing agricultural production and productivity have been compounded by the strong preference in rural areas for subsistence activities rather than wage employment on plantations.

In the South Pacific the plantation system has not developed to the extent that it has in the Caribbean. Although Browne and Scott (1989) appear to be critical of the lack of extension of the plantation system in the South Pacific, the social advantages of such extension would seem to be dubious. Whereas small holdings can be integrated into traditional communal life, commercial plantations involving wage employment cannot. Commercial plantations appear to be destructive of traditional communal life. The small holder, unlike the wage-earner, has the option of not being entirely dependent on cash income for survival. His family can, for example, grow some subsistence crops on their small holding. Thus they have more security than a wage-earner.

Most plantations are involved in monoculture and use artificial fertilizers and pesticides, all of which can be ecologically damaging. They are likely to be much more dependent upon imported inputs than are small holdings and are more vulnerable to trade variations. Furthermore, although greater weed control is generally achieved on plantations, this may be at the expense of greater soil erosion. So one can see the balance of the argument is not necessarily all one way in favor of plantations and the efficient modern technologies used by them.

Again small holdings may be favored on income distribution grounds even if plantations have some efficiency advantages. When plantations are owned by foreign interests or by wealthy local individuals, profits may be invested not in the country but abroad or used for consumption purposes. Higher returns may be obtained by investing these profits abroad, but this will do little to assist development of the island economy itself. In extreme cases, plantations give rise to a dual agricultural economy, with the plantation sector having little positive interaction with the local economy and with income distribution and land ownership being very unequal.

Many developing island economies rely heavily on tree crops for cash income. These have some advantages in that they do not require as intensive and as continuous application of inputs as annual crops. But trees often take many years before they bear. Furthermore, production from them cannot be so quickly adjusted to market demand as in the case of annual crops. In planting a tree crop, one often has to predict demand ten or more years in advance. This can be difficult to do with precision. In the short term, the supply of produce from tree crops is relatively inelastic, and the prices of such crops are therefore liable to very great fluctuations, e.g., consider the extent of fluctuations in coffee prices.

Most developing countries involved in the export of products from tree crops have tried to stabilize the prices paid to producers via government intervention. In the South Pacific "publicly owned commodity boards have been established to purchase and market the main export crops and, in most cases, to operate intervention schemes to counter the impact of fluctuations in world market prices on producer prices" (Browne and Scott, 1989, 8). But in times of boom, growers have put political pressure on commodity boards to increase prices, and boards have often been faced, as a result, with a shortage of stabilization funds to support prices during depressed conditions. This has frequently meant during that time that some support has been required from the general government budget. Overall this support provides a subsidy to this sector, that is to the commercial agricultural export sector.

In the South Pacific (and in Micronesia), much land is communal land, unlike in the Caribbean. Communal land ownership is believed to be a major impediment to agricultural growth and investment (cf., Fairbairn, 1985, 79). Banks, in giving credit, usually only do so on land for which there is a transferable title. This has tended to favor commercial private properties and plantations in the allocation of bank loans. Both legislation and traditional practice make it extremely difficult to transfer or lease communal land, and there are often land ownership disputes between villagers and tribal groups. However, traditional sharing arrangements tend to create greater equality in the distribution of income than otherwise might be the case. In the Caribbean, however, communal land does not appear to exist, and land ownership can show great inequality. But, even in the South Pacific, considerable inequality in land distribution is claimed to exist, and there is shortage of available land (Connell, 1988, 37).

Significant land shortages are claimed to exist in Tonga, the Cook Islands, Kiribati, and, to a lesser extent, in Fiji and Western Samoa. In many islands, all the land suitable for agriculture and forestry is being used for that purpose. However, in Papua New Guinea, Solomon Islands, and possibly Vanuatu, land is still available to be brought into economic production (Fairbairn, 1985, 7). But even in these larger island states, severe land shortages are present in some regions, for example, in the Highlands of Papua New Guinea. Growing land shortages have also been emphasized by Brookfield and Ward (1988, 49).

Concerning aspects of land distribution and income distribution, Brookfield and Ward (1988, 52–55) argue convincingly that traditional socioeconomic relationships are disintegrating in the South Pacific and that new elites are emerging. They suggest that changing systems of land allocation, coupled with social changes, not to mention shortages of land in some cases, are key factors in new differences in incomes. They go on to say, "The change from production of perishable food crops for on-farm consumption to marketed crops opens obvious avenues for accumulation and reinvestment. The unequal distribution of land rents amongst the members of owning groups on the basis of ascribed rank is another avenue" (Brookfield and Ward, 1988, 54).

Although Browne and Scott (1989) argue that governments in the South Pacific islands have favored subsistence agriculture in comparison to plantations, Connell (1988) argues that commercial crops, especially export crops, and plantations have on balance been favored by government policies. Connell's viewpoint also seems to be shared by Fairbairn (1985) who says, "Except in Fiji, Solomon Islands, Kiribati and Tuvalu, where the need to improve the standard of subsistence farming is a specific objective in planning documents, this sector has been largely neglected by development plans despite the fact that it embraces the great majority of rural inhabitants" (Fairbairn, 1985). In addition to the policies mentioned above as favoring commercial agriculture, subsidies for fertilizers and pesticides and on transport do likewise.

Fisk (1986) has stated that agriculture, like any other industry in Pacific island countries, is constrained by economic disadvantages of small scale, remoteness of world markets, and, in many cases, by transport problems due to extreme dispersal of islands or rugged terrain as in many parts of Papua New Guinea. He also claims that agricultural development planning has tended to neglect the mixed subsistence/cash subsector, which is the largest source of food, employment, and, in his view, export.

Although there is scope for further agricultural development in developing island states, such development does not appear to hold great promise for substantially reducing their dependence on foreign aid. At least in the Pacific, there seems to be a strong case for development planners giving greater attention to the subsistence and small holding agricultural sectors in their planning. In doing this, however, there appears to be a social case to avoid urban bias and prejudice in favor of cash incomes compared to income obtained from nonmarket sources. The case for integrated rural development is strong in the case of developing island microstates.

11

Further Issues in Natural Resource Utilization

As pointed out in the previous chapter, the production of developing island microstates is natural resource intensive. This is so despite the fact that many, possibly most, small states are not well endowed with natural resources. This is particularly so of island nations consisting of coral atolls. The resources in the sea and marine areas surrounding island states constitute one of their main natural resources. In this chapter, microstates' economic utilization of their fish, forest, and mineral resources is discussed.

The countries of the South Pacific have economic rights to a vast area of ocean. With the introduction of the 200-mile Exclusive Economic Zone (EEZ) following the Law of the Sea Convention, these countries, including Papua New Guinea, the Trust Territory of the Pacific Islands, and the Federated States of Micronesia, have rights over approximately 13 million square kilometers of ocean. In particular in most cases the ocean area controlled is vast both in relation to the land mass of island countries and their levels of population. The EEZ of Kiribati exceeds 1.3 million square miles, whereas its land mass is only 266 square miles and its population is about 65,000. The Federated States of Micronesia have an EEZ of more than 1.1 million square miles, a land mass of 271 square miles, and a population of about 91,000.

Two observations can be made. First, even if the oceans of these EEZs have low productivity of biomass per unit area (as is usual in tropical areas), total fish productivity is large given the size of the ocean area involved. Second, most developing island states face a daunting task in trying to enforce their exclusive property rights in the EEZ because of the very large area involved and their lack of surveillance equipment, vessels, and aircraft for enforcement. In some cases, these island states rely on the aid of friendly nations for enforcement, e.g., Australia and New Zealand, but enforcement remains patchy. Nevertheless, most island states see their fishery resources as a most valuable asset, a means to provide them with greater economic independence, and a source of additional funds for economic development. Fishery resources are best discussed in terms of onshore, or coastal fisheries, and offshore fisheries. Let us consider offshore fisheries first.

The principal fishery resource of the offshore areas of the South and Central Pacific islands is tuna, which consists of migratory species. Most of the developing island nations are not in a position to exploit this resource and other offshore fishery resources directly. These are, in fact, being exploited by the distant-water fishing fleets of larger nations, especially Japan and the United States, but also including the Philippines, South Korea, and Taiwan.

Island microstates, for several reasons, are not directly exploiting their tuna resources offshore. Except for the inhabitants of Kiribati, the islanders have little experience with offshore fisheries and little desire to stay away from home for long periods of time. Second, there are economies of scale in offshore operations, and the capital cost of ships and equipment is large. Third, they do not have as ready access to overseas markets as many of the larger more developed distant-water fishing nations do. Many lack the management skills and maintenance skills involved in operating a tuna fleet successfully.

Waugh (1989) has argued that South Pacific states will maximize their potential benefits from tuna in their 200-mile EEZ "if the specialist foreign nations harvest and process the majority of the catch, the Islands collect the resource rent as a fee for the fishing rights" (quoted in Joint Committee on Foreign Affairs, Defence and Trade, 1989, 19). On the one hand, this may enable the islands to extract the largest surplus if competition for fishing rights by foreign nations is relatively perfect and if agreements are faithfully fulfilled. On the other hand, fishing operations by foreign vessels may involve little or no direct interaction with the local economy and little direct local employment generation. Furthermore, such operations may provide no opportunities for islanders to learn by doing, and they will be deprived of opportunities to gather information directly about the extent of their deepwater fishery resources and the rate of exploitation of these resources by nations licensed to fish in their EEZ. In the last respect, SINs are dependent on information provided by the licensed fishing nations, and there is scope for cheating.

In addition to the above, much depends, from a development point of view, on the use made of the natural resource rent collected. If it is used for consumption purposes rather than for production investment, it may do little to develop an island economy. For example, it may be used mostly for public service employment and be spent mostly on imported consumption goods. Hence, little more than a single round of employment generation may result from the resource rent. In their effects, natural resource rents collected by the government may be very similar to foreign aid, which is used mainly to support public service employment in the islands. "Exploitation of these [tuna] resources is presently the monopoly of foreign fishing companies with island countries, notably Fiji, Papua New Guinea, Vanuatu, the Solomon Islands, Tonga and Tuvalu involved in a small way" (Fairbairn, 1985, 9). Fairbairn goes on to say, "Tuna processing is carried out in the first four of these countries, but in American Samoa tuna canning operations are substantial relying mostly on catches from foreign vessels."

Some of the tuna canneries are operated as joint ventures, e.g., the cannery in the Solomon Islands is owned jointly by Japanese interests and the government of the Solomon Islands. Although joint ventures can be advantageous to island countries, doubts have been raised about the extent to which SINs do, in fact, benefit from joint fishery ventures. For example, Doulman (1989) points out that by having governments as joint venturers, the foreign partner may receive valuable concessions and contacts (cf., Tisdell, 1989b). In many cases there is little transfer of skill. Top managers are often provided by the foreign partner, and local individuals may have little knowledge of the business operations of the company. For example, transfer pricing may be engaged in, and/or the volume of exports, for example, to the foreign parent of the joint venturer may be deliberately understated. Even where government representatives on the board of the joint venture come to know of such practices, they may fail to expose these for fear of creating embarrassment for the island government. But in most cases government appointments to the boards of joint ventures are political appointments, and the appointees have little knowledge of accounting and commercial practices.

Despite a global recession in the tuna industry in the 1980s, certain economic changes have benefitted Pacific island nations. Traditional tuna fishing grounds have shifted from the eastern Pacific to the central and western Pacific. Tuna plants have closed in the continental United States leaving more scope for supplies to be obtained from developing countries (Morrison, 1987, 62).

Most South Pacific island states have expected substantial economic gains from foreign harvesting of their offshore fishery resources. In practice, the extent of actual gains, the nature and fulfillment of agreements, and the extent of adherence to agreements and international conventions have been a source of controversy. Foreign fish harvesting is likely to continue to raise controversial issues for island nations.

The failure of the United States to recognize the property rights of island nations in migratory fish within their 200-mile limit (EEZ) but beyond their territorial waters precipitated political action on the part of southern Pacific islands. In 1985, Kiribati signed a one-year agreement with the Soviet Union permitting the USSR to fish in its EEZ; in 1987 Vanuatu signed a similar agreement. Just before the agreement between Kiribati and the USSR, the Solomon Islands seized the U.S. tuna boat *Jeanette Diana* for unlicensed fishing in its territorial waters. During this period South Pacific island states felt considerable hostility toward the U.S. attitude and the U.S. failure to pay royalties on its tuna catch in EEZs in the region.

With the signing of the agreement between the USSR and Kiribati, the United States recognized that, unless Pacific countries obtained adequate returns on their fishing resources, this might provide more scope for Soviet activity in the South Pacific. Accordingly, the United States and member nations of the Forum Fisheries Agency (FFA) signed a multilateral treaty whereby US $60 million is to be distributed to FFA members over a five-year period on a pro-rate basis according to catch in their respective EEZs.

Following this agreement, pressure was put on Japan to enter into a multilateral agreement with FFA. Japan has entered into bilateral agreements but has resisted entering into multilateral fishing agreements in the region.

Developments regarding royalties for fishing show that small island states can sometimes make gains by playing off the international political interests of larger developed nations. This has happened both in the Pacific and the Caribbean.

While the offshore fish of island microstates are a valuable resource, some island states have been overoptimistic about the value of offshore fish and about the maximum royalties they can expect to receive from their harvesting. Furthermore, these resources are not inexhaustible. They are renewable resources, but they become nonrenewable if they are overharvested and if breeding stocks are reduced below a critical mass. Because tuna are migratory and cross national boundaries, international cooperation by microstates may be necessary to prevent overharvesting of their partially shared tuna resources. Currently no such agreement covers international cooperation of this type in the central and southwest Pacific.

Inshore fisheries are the most heavily exploited fisheries of the developing island microstates. They play a major role in the subsistence economies of the Pacific. According to Fairbairn (1985, 9), accessible reef and lagoon areas are experiencing pressure from growing populations. He goes on to point out that exploiting such areas has become common, suggesting the need to explore the potential of "out-reef fishing and aquaculture" (Fairbairn, 1985, 9). "Several of the bigger countries, such as Papua New Guinea and the Solomon Islands, are more favored in having extensive 'shelf' areas, valuable not only for fishing but also as breeding grounds for marine life" (Fairbairn, 1985, 9).

As a result of increased harvesting pressures, many reef-dwelling species have become locally extinct, and many are being harvested beyond maximum sustainable yield rates and even beyond rates that will permit renewability. In many parts of the Central and South Pacific, for example, various species of giant clams have become locally extinct, and there is considerable harvesting pressure on the other species such as beche-de-mer or sea cucumbers. In the Caribbean, a number of species of sea turtles are endangered because of overharvesting and overcollecting of eggs. Both giant clams and sea turtles have been the subject of innovative programs aimed at their aquaculture and conservation.

In the Pacific islands, reef and ocean areas adjoining coastal villages have traditionally been claimed as communal property by villagers. To the extent that such arrangements still apply to coastal areas in the Pacific, they appear to have retarded the introduction of aquaculture. Aquaculture is, for instance, much less well established in the Pacific islands than in the Philippines. However, this is not due only to differences in property rights in marine resources.

In the Caribbean fishing does not enjoy a major role in the economies of many small island states. Some islands actually import substantial quantities of fish. In Jamaica, for instance, salt cod imported from the North Atlantic is actually a part of what might be considered the national dish. The taste for cod dates from the days of plantations based upon slavery, when that item was a staple in the diet of the slaves. Certainly a case could be made for import substitution with respect to cod, but to succeed it would have to overcome a historical preference of several centuries. Jamaica is not alone in the practice of importing fish; varieties of canned seafood can be found in food stores throughout the region.

In St. Vincent and the Grenadines, "Fish and fishery products are being imported, although St. Vincent exports fish to nearby islands, mainly because of poor internal marketing facilities, such as chilling facilities and flake ice supplies" (World Bank, 1985f, 14). On a policy level the World Bank suggested, "Efforts should be made to exploit the country's tremendous potential in this sector to substitute for imports and for further exports" (1985f, 19).

The situation in St. Vincent typifies conditions in many of the smaller Caribbean jurisdictions. With respect to St. Lucia, the World Bank suggested that nothing prevents that country from being self-sufficient in fish (World Bank, 1985e, 25). The same report referred to the absence of storage facilities but indicated that that particular situation had been rectified by the establishment of a facility which permitted storage of the surplus from the January–June season for use in the low season (1985e, 25). The low season, the report explained, was occasioned by fishermen being unable to go far out to sea because most are not equipped for deep-sea operations. Another issue exposed by the report is an excessive use of dugouts, which, aside from being inefficient, "has taken a toll on the forestry reserves" (1985e, 25). The report called for additional storage facilities to service parts of the country as well as for ramps to facilitate putting boats in the water (1985e, 25).

The lack of capital equipment appears to be a serious hindrance to the fishing industry among the smaller islands of the Caribbean. This problem involves not only storage and processing facilities but also fishing craft. A World Bank study of St. Christopher and Nevis found a depletion problem within three miles of shore that could be surmounted by the "adoption of more advanced fishing techniques [which] will allow exploitation of larger fish stocks located farther offshore" (1985d, 12). In some cases the microstates in question may be too small to realize economies of scale with respect to supplying fish for local markets.

One way around problems of scale would be international cooperation. Writing on that issue, William Demas called for regional collaboration, "whether by our countries allowing nationals of other CARICOM states to fish freely in their territorial waters and their Exclusive Economic Zones or by the formation of intra-regional joint ventures to exploit fishing grounds" (Demas, 1988a, 185). Demas recognized the potential of the fishing sector "for reducing expenditure on imports and for increasing export earnings" (1988a, 187). In regard to exports he saw particular potential in shrimp and lobster. Although enlarging EEZs has increased potential fishing areas, the industry is hampered by "a relatively large number of small-scale artisanal fishermen which together with storage and marketing problems" limits the extent to which the increased potential can be exploited (Demas, 1988a, 187). Demas decried the "underdevelopment of the modern trawler fishing industry," pointing out that fishing trawlers from many countries of the world operate within the EEZs of the microstates in question (Demas, 1988a, 187–88).

Forests are not a major natural resource of all island countries, but timber is a major export of a number of larger island nations in the Pacific. In the South Pacific, Papua New Guinea is the major commercial timber producer followed by the Solomon Islands. Fiji, Tonga, Vanuatu, and Western Samoa have smaller forestry industries, and Fiji has some plantations. But in other island states, such as atoll nations like Kiribati, timber and fuelwood are in extremely short supply.

Foreign-owned firms dominate the forestry industry of the South Pacific islands, and in most cases they are clearing tropical forests (rain forests) (e.g., in Papua New Guinea and Solomon Islands) to satisfy demand for specialist timbers in developed countries. They are contributing to the disappearance of rain forests and associated species, as has been emphasized by conservation groups. Most of the timber is exported in the form of logs, which means there is little value-added processing of timber in the islands from which it is obtained (Joint Committee on Foreign Affairs, Defence and Trade, 1989, 23). In many cases logs can be more easily transported than sawn timber, e.g., they can be floated to convenient loading points for shipping, but the lack of timber processing means the industry generates little employment in the Pacific island countries.

Apart from genetic loss due to felling forests, clearfelling in high rainfall areas results in soil erosion. In some areas, e.g., the Solomon Islands, clearfelling leads to serious soil erosion.

There have also been complaints of timber companies misleading customary owners about the amount of royalties they might expect to receive from the logging of their land. In some cases, too, timber companies have understated their profits so as to reduce royalty payments to customary owners (Joint Committee on Foreign Affairs, Defence and Trade, 1989, 23).

In the Caribbean, Haiti has experienced serious erosion damage because of deforestation. Speaking of CARICOM states, Demas pointed out "the Region has become more profligate in the abuse and underutilization of its forest resources to the extent that in a number of the countries the position is approaching crisis point" (Demas, 1988a, 188). He referred to "the widespread practice of burning and shifting cultivation [which] has resulted in the devastation of large areas of forest throughout the Region, seriously impairing the effectiveness of many water catchment areas" (Demas, 1988a, 188). The results have included extensive erosion, silting, regular flooding, declining stream flow, and "an inexorable decline of soil fertility," which have collectively resulted in

significant declines in agricultural yields that are difficult to reverse"
(Demas, 1988a, 188).

Forestry involving selective logging of natural stands, and, in some
cases, replanting may be the best available commercial use of some land
areas (e.g., land unsuitable for agriculture) in island states. But attention
needs to be given to sustainable harvesting of forests and any environmental spillovers from logging.

A limited number of island states have minerals that are currently
being mined or that are suitable for commercial development. Papua New
Guinea and New Caledonia are considered to be mineral rich (Joint Committee on Foreign Affairs, Defence and Trade, 1989, 23). As pointed out
in the previous chapter, minerals are the major export of Papua New
Guinea. Gold, copper, and silver are important mineral exports of Papua
New Guinea; nickel is an important export for New Caledonia; and gold
is a sizable export in value terms for Fiji. But, except for phosphate
deposits, most coral atolls have no minerals of commercial value.

In the Caribbean, Jamaica has sizable bauxite reserves, but the export
demand for that mineral has fallen on hard times in recent years. This has
occurred even though Jamaican bauxite "had a very low silica content and
was easy to mine, involving little more than scraping the material off the
top of the local terrain" (Manley, 1987, 19). Bauxite deposits also exist in
the Dominican Republic, Haiti, and the U.S. Virgin Islands (Barry et al.,
1984, 110–12). Beyond bauxite the Caribbean islands are not a major
source of minerals. The Dominican Republic produces some ferro-nickel
as well as gold and silver (Barry et al., 1984, 110).

Phosphate deposits are mined for fertilizer. In the Pacific, they were
mined from Ocean Island in Kiribati and are still being mined from
Nauru. Within a few years the deposit in Nauru will be mined completely
as was the deposit on Ocean Island. The Nauruans have the highest per
capita income of Pacific islanders, but the source of that income will
disappear within a few years, and their island will have been virtually
mined away. In order to provide income after mining operations cease,
Nauru has invested some income abroad. It remains to be seen whether
the income from this investment will be sufficient to support Nauruans
and provide them with a satisfying life. The Nauruans have not been able
to develop any domestic industry to sustain them after the cessation of
mining operations. In relation to mining, the Joint Committee on Foreign
Affairs, Defence and Trade (1989, 22), notes that "minerals are not an
infinite resource and other areas of the economy need to be developed in
conjunction with mining to provide an alternative source of export
earnings should the deposits run out."

Mining is a relatively capital-intensive industry, generating little local employment. Major mining operations in developing island economies are in the hands of foreign companies, even though joint venture arrangements exist, e.g., between the government of Papua New Guinea and Australian companies involved in the Bougainville copper mine and in the Ok Tedi gold and copper mine.

Mining operations can be very disruptive of local communities. The influx of foreigners to assume major roles in developing and operating a mine often brings sudden socioeconomic change. Furthermore, the mine may directly displace local inhabitants or lead to environmental effects that undermine their traditional livelihood. For example, it has been reported that copper mining in Bougainville has increased the sediment greatly in the local river and has reduced possibilities for fishing by the local people. Possibly partially as a result of social disruption caused by the mining operations in Bougainville, a secessionist group is now active on the island, has sabotaged mining installations, and has killed a number of people. The mine has been closed until law and order is restored.

The Ok Tedi gold and copper mine is being developed in the remote Highlands of Papua New Guinea. Moving equipment to the site has been difficult and much has had to be flown in by helicopter. A community until recently a Stone Age community is thus being brought suddenly into close, direct contact with a technologically advanced society. Undoubtedly there will be considerable local social impact, some of which will be adverse. It will be difficult for local individuals to retain control over their local affairs and environment. Their community may no longer be sustainable. It has also been reported that this mining operation will have some adverse environmental effects farther afield. Sediments and heavy metals are likely to enter the Fly River, a major river in Papua New Guinea, and this could have adverse effects on productivity of the river and on the health of individuals. Consuming produce from the river and in the marine areas surrounding its outlet could involve a health hazard. Although such reports may be exaggerated, environmental impacts from mining need to be seriously considered in evaluating any development proposal for minerals.

Foreign interests appear to be able to place natural resource extraction activities, such as logging, commercial fishing, and mining, into under-developed traditional societies with relative ease. The extent to which these frontier industries can penetrate even remote communities is amazing. The dangers with such frontier activities are that they may irretrievably damage the environment and that companies engaged in this may pay little attention to the social fabric of local communities. Furthermore, in some cases these communities appear to be exploited as advantage is taken of the comparative ignorance of local people, e.g., locals may be paid lower royalties than is reasonable or the profit or production of foreign companies may be understated to reduce royalty payments or promises may not be kept.

In the Pacific islands, and in most other underdeveloped island microstates, commercial fishing, forestry, and mining are heavily dependent on direct foreign investment. The produce from such activities is usually intended for foreign markets in developed countries. Although these activities may have few economic linkages with the host country (especially since value added and the extent of processing are often minimal), social and environmental impacts may be far from minimal. Also host countries often tend to remain dissatisfied with their share of gains from such resource exploitation. Such dissatisfaction may or may not be warranted; nevertheless, the situation does lend itself to "politicization" and can give rise to continuing international conflict about the equity of sharing arrangements.

12

Conservation and the Environment

Given the obvious impacts of economic growth on the environment in recent times, it has become increasingly clear from an environmental point of view that the world is a global village. Today economic change and growth have global environmental effects as well as localized ones. Although the global environmental impact of economic developments in small island states is likely to be small, economic developments in the rest of the world and changes wrought by larger nations pose substantial environmental threats to island microstates. As discussed below, the future survival of many SINs is threatened by the possibility of sea level rises. It has been argued that the release of various gases, especially carbon dioxide from using fossil fuels in economic activity in developed countries, is causing rising temperatures that threaten to melt the polar ice caps and cause sea level rises.

Yet it would be incorrect to believe that the environmental degradation of small island countries is without consequences for the rest of the world. If production from living natural resources and living things is to be sustained, their environmental life-support systems must be maintained. As indicated in the two previous chapters, developing island microstates are heavily dependent on living resources to sustain their inhabitants. Any environmental degradation that reduces the productivity of these living resources will reduce the earned income of islanders and lead either to demands for a greater amount of aid from aid donors or pressure to migrate to more developed countries or both. Second, to the extent that produce is exported from small island states to the rest of the world, especially the developed world, e.g., tuna and timber, these supplies may be reduced (and prices may rise) if desirable conservation practices are not followed or if unwanted environmental changes occur. Third, small islands are exotic places for tourists from more developed larger countries, and their attractiveness depends to a large extent on the conservation of their special environment. Fourth, many islands have unique species, which have evolved in relative isolation. These have curiosity value as well as potential economic value, e.g., for global medicinal use. Hence, it is incorrect to believe that conservation of the environment of small islands or the reverse is without consequence for the rest of the world.

In discussing this topic, let us first consider the adverse environmental impacts on island microstates originating from the rest of the world, mainly developed countries. Then let us consider the implications of internal developments of microstates for the state of their environment. In addition let us pay attention to the natural environmental hazards island nations face and briefly consider projects (such as those for the mariculture of giant clams) designed to promote resource conservation and sustainable use of resources.

Although there is considerable uncertainty about the actual nature of the "greenhouse effect," about the rate of climatic change that may flow from it, and the extent and rate of sea level changes that may stem from it, growing global concern is being expressed about this possibility, which an increasing number of scientists agree is not only possible but probable. This effect is mainly attributed to the release of gases as a result of economic activity, especially in developed economies. These gases include carbon dioxide and those reducing the protective ozone layer. What is clear is that a rise in sea levels of even modest proportions will have disastrous consequences for many SINs. This will certainly be the case for low-lying coral islands and sandy cays. Crocombe (1989, 1) points out that "estimates like a one-meter increase [in the sea level] in 40 years would make most atolls uninhabitable in their present form, because what matters is not the general sea level but the level in times of vulnerability during spring tides, hurricanes, tsunamis, etc. and the reduction of the fresh water lens."

In the Pacific, Kiribati, the Marshall Islands, Tokelau, and Tuvalu are countries that are likely to be very seriously affected by sea level rises. Indeed, they may end up with no habitable land, and their inhabitants may become ecological refugees, the survival of whom may depend on the opportunity to migrate to larger countries. In the Caribbean region, the Bahamas, the Turks and Caicos, Bermuda (which is actually in the Atlantic), and the Cayman islands would be very seriously impacted, as would low-lying areas of various other islands. Even small increases in sea level are likely to lead to serious erosion of low-lying atolls and may cause salinization of the water lenses that underlie them and are an important source of fresh water.

Nuclear contamination is also an issue for many island states, especially those in the Pacific. The Pacific islands have been the scene of nuclear tests by the United States, Britain, and France. Between 1946 and 1963 the United States conducted 103 tests in the Marshall Islands, Johnson Islands, and Christmas Islands. Since 1967, France has conducted more than 127 nuclear tests in the Tuamotu Islands of French Polynesia. Concern about exposure to nuclear risks in the Pacific has led to a Nuclear Free Pacific Movement, and the governments of New Zealand, Vanuatu, and Palau have declared their countries nuclear free. Reports of ill health as a result of nuclear testing in the Pacific are not infrequent. Islanders from the atoll of Rongolap in the Marshall Islands, for instance, blame a legacy of leukemia, miscarriages, birth defects, and thyroid tumors on a nuclear bomb dropped by the United States in 1954 on Bikini atoll 160 km. away (Anon, *Pacific Islands Monthly,* August 1988, 14).

Despite the concerns of Pacific islanders about nuclear testing, France continues with it. This has been "attributed to the continuing 'moral' support of Britain and the U.S., as well as the ineffectiveness of forces of opposition" (Herrman, 1989, 36). Herrman suggests "most Pacific Islands are limited in resources, economies are linked to the world economy, they are dependent on aid and militarily weak. Under these conditions, economic consideration for political survival inevitably receives priority government attention. Thus it is difficult to make principled stands on issues" (Herrman, 1989, 36).

Another matter of concern among islanders is larger nations dumping toxic wastes in sea areas near them and the possibility of their land areas being used as dumps for toxic wastes from industrialized countries. There was, for example, widespread concern in 1980 when Japan proposed dumping low-level radioactive waste south of the Mariana Islands in the Pacific Ocean. According to Twyford (1988, 48), waste companies are beating a path to island governments to find a place to dispose of industrial wastes. "Five South Pacific nations have been approached by United States companies seeking waste disposal sites but as yet none have been swayed by the jobs, cash and other lures offered by the waste company entrepreneurs." In Tonga, a great amount of controversy erupted when Princess Salote Piloleva Tuita became a shareholder in a waste disposal company that planned to accept one container load of toxic waste a day from California for incineration. It was said that PCBs, asbestos, or dioxins were to be imported. Despite the pressure brought to bear by some members of the royal family on the government, this proposal was eventually rejected. In recent times, the president of the

Marshall Islands also caused controversy when he asked the United
States to consider storing high level radioactive waste in the Marshalls in
return for a large compensation payment. From the point of view of
developed countries, the remoteness of many islands from large metropolitan centers makes them attractive dumping grounds for toxic wastes.
But the ecosystems of such islands tend to be fragile, and, because those
islands are small, their residents are unlikely to escape the ill effects of
any mishaps that occur in toxic waste disposal on these islands. Inhabited
islands would take considerable risks in becoming waste disposal dumps.
Twyford (1988, 48) comments, "The thrust into the Pacific coincides
with a worldwide move by waste companies in the West to dump their
refuse on developing nations." It might also be noted that many of these
countries still continue to import and use may types of pesticides that
have been banned in developed countries because of their adverse environmental effects.

Although not all islands are near major shipping routes, many run the
risk of oil spills from passing tankers or other ships. The Caribbean is at
special risk in this regard because the region is replete with refining
facilities. In addition it experiences heavy traffic because of the Panama
Canal and busy southern ports in the United States. In the Pacific region
there is also a temptation for ships to discharge unwanted oil in the EEZs
of island countries because their EEZs are so large and because they are
not in a position, as a rule, to detect such violations.

The fishing techniques used by distant-water fishing nations have
also been a matter of concern for a number of island countries. Some of
the techniques sweep the ocean clean and capture unwanted animals. For
example, gill netting is used to catch albacore tuna in international waters
in the Pacific. Gill nets are up to 56 km. long and designed to drift in the
ocean. Apart from catching albacore tuna, "the nets also catch sea birds,
dolphins, and even small whales — which led to the nets being dubbed
the 'wall of death' — but the most immediate problem is that most of the
catch is in the form of juvenile albacore tuna. This has resulted in the
depletion of the tuna numbers of adult fish in the economic zones of the
Forum states" (Anon, *South Pacific Islands Monthly,* June 1989, 31).
Consequently, many small nations find the albacore tuna within their
EEZs dwindling and are likely to suffer economic loss as a result.

Other ways in which developed countries have adverse environmental
impacts on developing island microstates include their demand for natural
resources, e.g., timber from rain forests, foreign investment in island
states causing adverse environmental effects, foreign aid that ignores the
environmental consequences of the activities supported, and foreign

tourism of an environmentally destructive nature. In principle it is within the province of island states to control or limit these effects, but some states may find this politically very difficult to do. Nevertheless, the above do not always have serious adverse environmental effects, or it may be that the net benefits obtained outweigh the environmental costs imposed.

Let us now consider conservation and environmental variations that arise mainly from domestic sources. Both population growth and increases in aggregate economic output can be powerful forces leading to environmental degradation, and, as elsewhere in the world, they are having an impact in small island states. The island countries of the central western and South Pacific have small land areas, but they have a big problem in common with many developing countries. "Nearly all have experienced high population growth rates of around 2 per cent or higher in the past few decades, threatening pressure on resources and escalation of social and economic stress" (Brookfield and Ward, 1988, 29). The higher growth rates occurred first in Polynesia, until relieved by out migration, and then occurred in Melanesia. Rates of population growth are now higher in parts of Melanesia than in countries in Africa and Asia. The islands of the Caribbean are also experiencing population pressure. Barbados has the highest population density in the Western Hemisphere.

Where such growth is not sufficiently relieved by out migration, it is placing increased pressure on the natural environment of island countries. In those countries with land areas as yet uncleared for cultivation, cultivation is extending at the expense of the natural environment, and harvesting of inshore fishery resources is intensifying to the extent that their productivity is being reduced and, in some cases, the local continuing existence of a number of species is threatened.

To some extent rural environmental pressures are relieved by the widespread movement of individuals in small island countries to urban areas. However, this also brings with it new environmental problems. Urban areas themselves completely destroy the natural environment and frequently use land that could have been productive for agricultural purposes, even though that might not necessarily be the best use for it. Any remaining natural resources close to urban areas tend to be exploited at unsustainable rates as locals attempt to supplement their incomes. It is no surprise that many marine species have become locally extinct in areas surrounding larger urban centers in island countries, e.g., giant clams around Nuakalofa in Tuvalu.

Urban areas also produce wastes, such as human excreta, in concentrations that in the natural environment are difficult to degrade and recycle quickly. Problems exist with the disposal of both liquid wastes and solid wastes. Much of the solid waste comes through exports from more developed countries, e.g., of food and drink in containers, and there is little economic scope for recycling it, even though "tip scavengers" in many developing countries ensure that much of this material is reused in ingenious ways.

Unless human wastes from urban areas are adequately treated, they become a vehicle for the spread of disease and can give rise to ill health where they contaminate water supplies. There are particular problems involved in waste disposal on atolls because these islands generally have fresh water lenses underground, no surface water. Apart from tanks, this underground water is the only supply of potable water. It can be contaminated by wastes, e.g., septic tanks. Even disposing of sewage by means of ocean outfalls is a problem. Such sewage is likely to kill coral in the vicinity of the outlet because of reduction in light caused by the sediment. It may also cause algal growth and pollute near-shore marine areas, for example, filter feeders such as mollusks, with adverse impacts on health. Such effects have, for example, been noted in Bali and in Thailand in areas of tourist development.

As mentioned in previous chapters, islands are geographically diverse and may be classified in a variety of ways. At a conference dealing with the environmental management of small islands organized by the U.S. Man and the Biosphere Program (United States Department of State, 1986), islands were divided into two sets — high islands and low islands and various broad generalizations made about the state of their natural environment and natural resource management.

Low islands usually suffer from water shortages. Water in Pacific low islands mainly comes from rainwater collected in tanks or from wells (underground supplies), and there are dangers of contamination and overuse. The high islands are mostly dependent upon running water for drinking, supplemented by supplies from tanks. As a result of forest clearing in high areas, the unregulated use of agrochemicals, and the disposal of wastes in rivers and streams, there is a danger of pollution (United States Department of State, 1986, 49).

The low islands in the Caribbean suffer from chronic water shortages, and underground water is easily contaminated. Water is imported or desalted in some areas. On the high islands, seasonal water shortages occur. Streams are subject to much variability in flow partially due to loss of natural vegetation cover, and flash flooding is a problem in lowland areas. Increasing populations in the Caribbean, as elsewhere, will place increasing pressure on water resources.

The low islands of the Pacific are extremely dependent on imported fuel for energy. The high islands depend on imported fuel supplemented by hydroelectric power. Use of firewood is widespread and is expected to increase and could result in deforestation. The situation is much the same in the Caribbean, but it is more dependent on imported fossil fuel.

Both in the Caribbean and the Pacific, there is cause for alarm about forests. In the Pacific there is a threat of virtual loss of all wood supplies on the low islands, and there is a scarcity of wood for domestic use. The few remaining extensive forests on high islands are rapidly disappearing as they are used for timber or encroached on by agriculture. "Indiscriminate clearing of forest areas is quite common, causing rapid loss of fertile soil, decreases in wildlife populations and contamination of water supply" (United States Department of State, 1986, 45). The position in the Caribbean is even worse with both high and low islands being wood importers. They face a serious timber shortage and suffer the adverse environmental impact of deforestation. This is also the case for the Mediterranean and North Atlantic islands.

In the Pacific islands there has been intensive overfishing inshore plus damage to fish from dynamiting, coral crushing, and poisoning water areas. As indicated previously, coastal urban pressures are resulting in increased destruction of coral and marine life. In some areas mining and forestry are leading to coastal ecological damage, for example, from greater discharge of sediments into the ocean. Both in the Caribbean and in the Pacific, the people depend heavily on imported canned fish, some of which in the latter case may be caught in their EEZs.

In the Pacific on those islands where shifting agriculture is practiced, population pressure has led to shifts growing and intensifying. This is resulting in increased loss of forests causing soil erosion and water pollution. Furthermore, "in most islands there is a lack of formal land-use plans, and most islands still operate under 'customary tenure.' Under such tenure land is often used for unsuitable purposes, e.g., agriculture instead of water catchment. Absence of proper land planning has given rise to overconcentration of deleterious activities in certain areas" (United States Department of State, 1986, 45).

Wildlife is under serious threat in nearly all island countries. On the low islands, wildlife has lost most of its natural habitat, and much has also disappeared on high islands. Invasions of exotic wildlife, including feral animals, have played havoc with native species on most islands. Furthermore, the increased availability of firearms coupled with easier means of transport to remote places has put increasing pressure on remaining wildlife. Feral cats, feral dogs, feral pigs, and introduced rats are especially destructive of island wildlife. For instance, the rats eat birds' eggs or chicks. Ground-dwelling small animals are at risk from feral dogs and pigs. Virtually all island countries are experiencing problems from introduced species that are threatening to eliminate many of their unique species. An unusual case is the brown tree snake *Boiga irregularis,* which was accidentally introduced to Guam from Melanesia. The snake is believed to have contributed to the virtual extinction of nine species of birds and to the serious reduction in a number of other species (North, 1989, 24). It is claimed that "having depleted its natural food supply in the jungled interior of the island, the brown tree snake is encroaching on the densely populated coastal areas, eating chicks, chicken eggs, small pets — even pet food — and entering houses" (North, 1989, 24).

While setting aside reserves or protected areas may help to conserve species, more positive action is needed in some cases. For example, measures must be taken to eradicate or control unwanted introduced species or to protect endangered species from them.

In some cases artificial breeding programs may assist. An interesting case in that respect is the mariculture or aquaculture of giant clams in the Pacific (Tisdell, 1986; 1989b; Copland and Lucas, 1988) and the culture of green turtles in the Caribbean. Both species are considered to be endangered at least locally.

Giant clams occur naturally only in the Indo-Pacific area and have been harvested by islanders for subsistence. As a result, however, of population increases, demand for clam meat in Asian markets, and improved technology, giant clams have disappeared from many areas in the Pacific (cf., Tisdell, 1983). All species have now been listed under the Convention on International Trade in Endangered Species, which restricts international trade in such species.

Experiments aimed at breeding giant clams in captivity began with U.S. assistance at the Micronesian Mariculture Demonstration Center in Palau. The species *Tridacna derasa* was first bred there in captivity, and the possibilities for farming it were explored. Subsequently other species were bred in captivity, and Australia began a project at James Cook University in northern Australia aimed at establishing techniques for the mariculture of *Tridacna gigas,* the largest of the giant clam species. Since then experimental stations have been established in the Philippines, Solomon Islands, Fiji, and other places.

The mariculture of giant clams holds out promise as a means to restock coral reefs in island countries depleted of clams, thus enabling islanders to once again supplement their diet with these delicacies high in protein content. Also, for some islands it may mean that a viable new commercial mariculture industry can be based on giant clams, given that sufficient demand exists abroad, especially in Asia. But the economics of such an industry have yet to be established. Giant clams do not need to be artificially fed or fertilized (many maricultured products do). For many SINs this is a positive factor because it means little import leakage. A further advantage of the mariculture of giant clams is that it is environmentally benign compared to shrimp culture in brackish coastal ponds. In addition, because of their symbiotic relationship with algae that grows on their mantle, giant clams thrive in coral environments and water that is not nutritionally rich provided they have adequate sunlight. Both Australia and the United States via Palau are distributing maricultured seed clams or brood stock to the Pacific Islands. In the Caribbean, partly as a result of British and German aid, the closed cycle mariculture of green turtles was established on the Cayman Islands. Unlike giant clam farming green turtle farming seems to require a larger scale of investment and may not be so suitable for introduction at village level. Nevertheless, a number of conservationists have supported such ventures on the basis that they reduce pressures on harvesting natural stock. The opponents argue that widespread availability of turtle meat, if mariculture of turtles expands, will result in greater demand for it (a shift upward in the demand curve) and place greater pressure on natural stocks. The issue has not been completely resolved (see Tisdell, 1986).

An environmental hazard, more common in the Caribbean than in the Pacific region, has been the advent of dirty manufacturing facilities. These run the gamut from oil refining to metal products, plastics, and pharmaceuticals. The nearness of Caribbean locations to mainland North American markets, coupled with the existence of a literate labor force, makes the islands attractive to industry. The firms themselves often find that the islands in question afford them the opportunity to avoid the potential of regulatory unpleasantness in Canada and the United States. Island states with such facilities would do well to pay careful attention to their environmental impacts.

In conclusion, not all environmental problems and hazards faced by island microstates are manmade. Many island microstates are located in areas where there is a high probability of natural disaster. Many are located in hurricane or cyclone belts, and tidal waves (tsunamis) are a risk in some. These can have disastrous consequences for small island states, which usually need the assistance of larger countries to deal with the emergency that arises in the aftermath of a natural disaster. Periodic droughts and fires are a hazard in some microstates (Connell, 1988, 36), and environmental health problems, such as malaria (strains of which are now resistant to modern drugs), occur in some island states (Simms, 1989). These natural environmental hazards also constrain the economic development of SINs.

IV
A Final Overview

13

Selected International Considerations

Most island economies exhibit a high degree of dependence on international trade given the way in which they have evolved. Furthermore, the less developed ones show lack of diversity in the composition and direction of their trade, and this makes them economically very vulnerable to external influences. This problem of external dependence is compounded by the substantial dependence of many on foreign aid (the major part of which comes as a rule from one or two donors), as well as by the importance of foreign direct investment in their nontraditional sectors. Foreign direct investment is especially important in their commercial sectors, such as the tourism and finance industries, import-export services, and a number of manufacturing and distribution activities. Consequently today most small island economies are very open to external economic influences. Let us consider in more detail aspects of their trade, foreign aid, international remittances, and foreign direct investment in them.

Whereas not all island countries in the South Pacific have high export ratios in relation to GDP, all have high import ratios. The larger island countries tend to have higher export ratios than the smaller ones. The smaller countries are more dependent on foreign aid and remittances to cover their trade deficits. In 1987 exports as a percentage of GDP at market prices were for Fiji 45%, for Papua New Guinea 44%, for the Solomon Islands 45%, and for Western Samoa 41%. In Tonga in 1987–1988 and in Vanuatu in 1987, exports were only a little over 11% of their GDP at market prices. For Kiribati in 1986 exports were only 7.7% of GDP at market prices. Imports for those countries in the same periods ranged from a low of 48% for the Solomon Islands and Vanuatu to a high of over 68% for Kiribati and over 100% for Tonga. If exports and imports are added together and expressed as a ratio of GDP (as is commonly done to measure trade dependence), all these island countries show a high degree of trade dependence. Those countries in this group that run substantial trade and services account deficits rely to a considerable extent on official transfers (foreign aid) or international private transfers (remittances) to cover them.

As discussed in previous chapters, the exports of many island countries consist mainly of primary products and most rely for the bulk of their export earnings on fewer than four products. In Fiji, for example, sugar is the mainstay of exports. As Fairbairn (1985, 38) points out, Pacific "island export development to date remains very much at the primary level. Expansion and diversification of exports has been impressive in several cases, but as a general rule export performance has been poor with some sharp declines." He was of the opinion that "island countries remain essentially at the 'hewer of wood' stage with unprocessed minerals, agricultural raw materials and foodstuffs of overriding importance." Value added to exported commodities through processing and semiprocessing tends to be low. For example, the bulk of timber exports from the Pacific islands is in the form of logs rather than sawn timber. Usually, it is more economical to process primary products (except to reduce bulk and transport costs) in or close to export markets rather than in underdeveloped island economies.

By comparison with larger countries, developing island economies lack appropriate skills, economies of size of enterprises and of industrial agglomeration, and, in some cases, adequate energy and water supplies needed for processing. Furthermore, the cost of transport within island economies can be high, e.g., where they consist of widely scattered islands such as Kiribati or where rugged terrain interferes with land transport as in Papua New Guinea. If raw materials need, for example, to be transported from outer islands to a central island or point for processing in the country, this will mean extra unloading and reloading costs as well as extra internal transport costs compared to the case where the raw materials can be directly transported from the outer islands to their export markets. In such circumstances, domestic processing can only be economical if there are substantial processing cost advantages in the island country compared to overseas destinations. But in most cases developing island countries do not have this advantage, which, when combined with the transport cost factor, helps to explain the low processed content of their exports.

Taking the less developed Pacific islands as a whole (including the Federated States of Micronesia and the French territories of French Polynesia and New Caledonia), minerals (mostly copper, nickel, gold, and phosphate) are major exports by value. However, this is principally so because of the large copper and gold exports of Papua New Guinea, the nickel exports of New Caledonia, and the phosphate exports of Nauru. Agricultural export products are more representative. These include coffee, cocoa, tea, kava, spices, and coconut products. Fish, shells, and handicrafts are also common exports, and, depending on the country, palm oil, sugar and molasses, timber and timber products. Fiji and the Cook Islands export some textiles and clothing. Actual export structures differ substantially even though most of the Pacific island countries are principally dependent on exports of primary products. Fairbairn (1985, Ch. 4) has classified these and points out that in the case of the smallest island countries "exports are at very low levels and tend to be dominated by such traditional staples as copra and handicrafts. The capacity to achieve further diversification is severely restricted by environmental and geographic factors" (Fairbairn, 1985, 431).

Recent data from the Caribbean region indicate that exports vary widely as a percentage of GDP from nation to nation. In Jamaica, for instance, exports are very important, registering 57% of GDP in 1988. In Trinidad they were somewhat less important at 35%. In Haiti and the Dominican Republic, they accounted for 19% and 20% of GDP, respectively.

In Barbados the relatively strong performance of the export sector was attributed to "higher sales of chemicals, food and clothing, mainly to the CARICOM market" (Inter-American Development Bank, 1989, 270). In the Dominican Republic "industrial free zone activities (whose net earnings are not included in the official GDP) added . . . 18,000 jobs" (Inter-American Development Bank, 1989, 317). In March 1989 free zone activity employed over 85,000 persons, and the "current domestic value added of these operations is estimated at almost 3 percent of GDP" (Inter-American Development Bank, 1989, 317).The report cited indicated that recent policy support for free zones has resulted in the establishment of electronics, assembly, and data entry operations employing higher skilled labor.

In the case of Haiti, the clothing industry, "the principal source of value added in the export-oriented assembly industry" was holding its own in 1988 while most other assembly operations suffered declines (Inter-American Development Bank, 1989, 357). In 1988 Haiti suffered a 23% decline in the dollar value of exports. Manufacturing exports were hard hit, falling by 37%. "Particularly affected were the exports of sporting goods, toys and electronic parts" (Inter-American Development Bank, 1989, 358).

Jamaica was hard hit by Hurricane Gilbert in 1988. The storm damaged an estimated 85% of industrial facilities and in particular the garment industry. "Despite these problems . . . the finishing of imported textiles for re-export to the United States still increased slightly to $103.4 million" (Inter-American Development Bank, 1989, 373).

The World Bank (1988, 5) reported that Caribbean countries lost about 20% of their share in the US-EEC-Canada markets during the period from 1980 to 1986. Causal elements in the situation included a greater dependence upon commodities with depressed prices, reductions in the U.S. sugar quota, and minor preferential treatment extended by the markets in question. In addition the report declared that "some Caribbean countries followed policies that hindered export growth" (1988, 5).

Among the most serious hindrances to export growth among Caribbean nations was their policy of pegging their currencies to the U.S. dollar. The result was "a real appreciation during the early 1980's against virtually all other export markets" (World Bank, 1988, 5). The result was reduced profitability "not only in their export markets, but also compared to their competitors" (1988, 5).

Most of the exports of Pacific island countries go to developed countries where they provide raw materials for manufacture. More than half the total exports of the Pacific islands go to Europe and Japan. Japan is the leading market and the fastest growing one, with France, the United States, and Australia being important export destinations. More than half the exports of the Solomon Islands go to Japan alone. The United States and Europe are major destinations for exports from Caribbean countries.

The destination of exports of Pacific islands tends to differ depending upon the historical colonial ties of the country. For example, most of American Samoa's exports go to the United States; those of the Cook Islands and Niue, to New Zealand; those of Kiribati, to the United Kingdom; and those of French Polynesia and New Caledonia, to France. But these traditional ties are weakening, and developed and developing Asian countries are making headway as destinations for the region's exports. For example, between 1970 and 1989, developing Asia-Pacific countries increased their share of the exports out of Fiji from 9.2% to 28.1%, from New Caledonia from 0.3% to 5.5%, Papua New Guinea from 0.9% to 9.7%, Tonga from 0% to 9.1%, and Solomon Islands from 1% to 15.2% (Morrison, 1987, 80).

However, trade between Pacific island countries remains low especially if reexports are excluded. Less than 3% of the exports of Pacific island countries enter intraregional trade if nonregional reexports are excluded (Fairbairn, 1985, 48). Intraregional domestic exports consist of raw materials sent to neighboring countries for processing, e.g., tuna to American Samoa and copra to Fiji; locally produced foodstuffs involving little processing, e.g., sugar and meat from Fiji, rice from the Solomon Islands, and fruits and vegetables from Tonga; and locally manufactured products of a nontechnical nature such as biscuits, metal goods, paint, and nails.

Pacific island countries have given much attention to trying to increase intraregional trade but progress has been slow. Standingford (1982) has identified a number of constraints to such trade expansion. Even in combination the total market the Pacific island microstates provide is small by world standards and cannot provide substantial economies in manufacturing. Long distances between many of the islands do not make it necessarily economical to supply them from another island in their group. Japan and Australia, for example, are closer to many of the western Pacific islands than the eastern Pacific islands are to the western ones. The United States is closer to the islands in the western Caribbean than are the eastern Caribbean islands to the western ones. Also, given existing transport routes, it is difficult to create new patterns of trade. Transport links tend to be to the metropolitan countries rather than between island countries. Also many island countries produce similar types of products, and this tends to restrict trade opportunities. Furthermore, tariff barriers sometimes limit intraregional trade. In the Pacific many island countries impose tariffs on imports with reciprocal concessions being extended to metropolitan countries. This tends to reinforce trade with metropolitan countries rather than between island countries.

While the possibility of forming a free trade area between Pacific island countries has been given some consideration, especially by Pacific Forum members, it seems that the economic gains to island countries may be small. A free trade area would involve removing tariffs and trade barriers between members and keeping trade barriers against nonmembers unchanged. But conditions among Pacific island countries do not appear to be favorable to strong trade creation between them, e.g., there is not much difference between the price of their products, and there are the transport cost problems referred to above (cf., Fairbairn, 1985, 250–54). Possibly Caribbean countries have moved closer to economic cooperation through CARICOM (Caribbean Community) than have the Pacific islands.

The major imports of Pacific island countries are machinery and transport equipment, fuel, foodstuffs, and manufactured goods with Australia being the largest supplier followed by France, the United States, Japan, and New Zealand. Imports from Japan have expanded at the fastest rate. Imports of machinery and manufactured goods tend to be the largest category of imports in the larger island economies whereas food, beverages, and tobacco are the most important category of imports in the smallest economies — Cook Islands, Kiribati, Nauru, Niue, Tokelau, and Tuvalu. Food dependence is also high in Cape Verde, Comros, Dominica, Grenada, St. Kitts-Nevis, St. Vincent, Sao Tome, and elsewhere (Connell, 1988, 37). In some cases island countries are purchasing food from their own region that has been processed abroad, e.g., tinned fish.

Most island economies run substantial trade deficits, and most have a considerable deficit on overall international transactions in products plus services. This deficit is usually covered by foreign aid payments or remittances from relatives overseas. Take Tonga, for example. In 1987–1988, it had a trade deficit of 61.7 million pa'anga and a net surplus in trade in services of 4.73 million pa'anga leaving a deficit of 56.97 million pa'anga. This was largely covered by net private remittances of 31.49 million pa'anga and official transfers (foreign aid) of 20.02 million pa'anga.

The Solomon Islands, however, because it had fewer migrants abroad, had much less dependence on private remittances as a balancing item. It also had a larger deficit on services, possibly because tourism is relatively underdeveloped in the Solomons. In 1987, the Solomon Islands had a trade deficit of 6.73 million Solomon Island dollars and a deficit on trade in services of 91.68 million Solomon Island dollars. This was financed principally by foreign aid, 83.4 million Solomon Island dollars, and to a minor extent by private remittances, 5.96 million Solomon Island dollars.

Let us consider some aspects of aid first and then discuss remittances. Aid per capita tends to be highest in the smallest microstates. Per capita foreign aid to island microstates is very high by world standards, especially in the Pacific (Connell, 1988, 76). Almost the total per capita income of the very small island countries in the Pacific, such as Kiribati, Tuvalu, Niue, and Tokelau, is accounted for by foreign aid. Connell (1988, 76) points out that aid to small island countries is "highest of all for territories that remain in a dependent relationship, notably the French overseas departments and territories. In nine states in the Pacific aid is equivalent to at least 50 percent of all income and in twelve is equivalent to over 50 percent of government expenditure." It is claimed that there is small-country bias in the aid giving of major donors.

The reasons for this seem to be varied. In some cases it is a matter of perceived strategic interest. To some extent this may have motivated President Reagan's Caribbean Basin Initiative. Japan has also increased her aid, partially to secure sources of raw material and natural resource supplies but also to help reduce its chronic balance of payments surpluses. Canada has also substantially raised its aid allocation to the Pacific region. To some extent this aid may be motivated by humanitarian considerations and a feeling that at least in a small state a donor can have a significant influence on per capita income whereas in a large and populous country such aid would be merely "a drop in the ocean." Although small more developed countries such as Australia and New Zealand can provide substantial visible aid to small island states, it is impossible for them to do so, for example, for larger countries such as Indonesia or India. In fact, the Jackson Report (1984) recommended that Australia try to concentrate its aid on small island countries in its region. The report also noted that small island countries have an equal vote in the General Assembly of the United Nations and hinted that this vote might be worth wooing with foreign aid policies.

Connell suggests that the economic effectiveness of foreign aid to microstates is not a critical issue for most major donors. He says, "For donors the real issue is delivery rather than performance. A high proportion of aid consequently goes in infrastructure provision, and this means 'technological bias' which has been criticized because of its urban bias, limited 'spread effects' and high maintenance costs" (Connell, 1988, 77–78).

In practice it seems, at least for the smallest Pacific islands, that foreign aid programs are principally disguised income transfer programs (cf., Tisdell, 1990). Howlett (1983) quoted in Connell (1985, 78) supports this view, indicating that many small island countries offer little scope for economic development. She indicated that development effort, assisted by aid, "has achieved little in reducing economic dependence, in stabilizing production and markets, in reducing or averting social crises or in bringing about a degree of balance between population and resources in the islands, although improvements in welfare have been achieved" (Howlett, 1983, 1).

Whatever doubts may be raised about the wisdom of relying on foreign aid (becoming economically dependent on it), there is no doubt that governments of SINs actively seek it. Most SINs pay lip service to the goal of becoming economically self-reliant, but this is not an achievable goal for many given their per capita income aspirations.

For many also the slogan "trade not aid" is empty, for, even with extremely favorable trade arrangements, many of the smallest underdeveloped microstates are so resource-poor that they would be unable to achieve a satisfactory level of per capita income. Nevertheless, more favorable trade arrangements with metropolitan countries may help island states reduce their dependence on foreign aid and are worth pursuing.

Remittances from migrants from small island countries are an important source of income and foreign exchange. For many Caribbean countries, remittances are the largest or second largest single source of foreign exchange and exceed foreign aid for most. In recent years, however, tourism has overtaken remittances as the largest single source of foreign exchange in several Caribbean countries, but remittances are still most important to the smallest countries. Depending upon the island nation concerned, remittances are a major source of foreign exchange earnings in the Pacific. This is so for Tonga, Cook Islands, Tuvalu, Western Samoa, American Samoa, and the Federated States of Micronesia.

Remittances appear to be used largely for consumption and nonproductive purposes (rather than for investment) or to enable other kin to migrate or to obtain further education with a view to migrating (Connell, 1988, 28). Connell (1988, 28) claims "migration and remittances have tended to create an appetite for the import of consumer goods, and hence expensive imports, which has driven up agricultural wages and therefore tended to squeeze that part of island microstates' economies with the most long-term productive promise." Brookfield and Ward (1988, 38) echo this point of view: "The inflationary effect of uncontrolled remittances can inhibit tourism and export growth. Through an increasing rate of consumption of imported consumer goods, particularly food, development of local agriculture and fishing industries can be slowed." They go on to say, "Used in this way, remittances encourage a progression from subsistence to stagnation and subsidy."

Remittances are an important source of foreign exchange that, despite the above difficulties, island governments welcome. But, because remittances tend to decline the longer a migrant stays abroad, it is necessary to maintain migration to sustain the inflow (Brookfield and Ward, 1988, 28; Connell, 1988, 29). It has also been argued that where migration is possible and leads to remittances, maintenance of fertility rates may result if education and reproduction costs are low. This is a rational economic response to the situation and appears to have occurred in some Pacific islands. (See studies quoted by Connell, 1988, 29.)

Another avenue for small island states to interact with the international economy is as recipients of foreign direct investment. Although foreign direct investment in the Pacific islands has been absolutely small in recent years, over time multinational corporations have come to dominate the key sectors of many island countries. Fairbairn and Parry (1986, 2) point out that this is especially so in "trading, mining, telecommunications, banking, insurance and the up-market hotels. Only in the fields of agriculture and small-scale business is significant local participation apparent." Recent direct capital investment in the Pacific islands has been dominated by inflows to Papua New Guinea, especially for mining; inflows to Fiji and the Solomon Islands have remained significant. But in the smaller islands, private capital inflows have been negligible (in some cases negative), indicating a lack of opportunities for profitable investment.

Australian-based multinational companies predominate in the South Pacific islands, but many of the Australian-based companies are branches or subsidiaries of United Kingdom and U.S. companies. However, in recent years there has been an increase in direct investment from the United States, Japan, and Southeast Asia in the region.

"Transnational corporations have penetrated the Caribbean more than other regions of the world" (Barry et al., 1984, 13). In fact, "Foreign capital dominates all the leading sectors of the region's economy: banking, tourism, mining, manufacturing, petroleum and export agriculture" (1984, 5). Barry and his colleagues go on to suggest that in certain industries (mining, local banking, agriculture, and utilities), many firms have transferred their stock ownership to host governments, while retaining influence through management contracts, technology transfer agreements, and marketing (1984, 17).

Most island states are heavily dependent on multinational corporations in their modern sectors, that is in sectors requiring relatively modern technology, management, marketing, or distribution skills. In some localized areas this gives mutlinational companies a monopoly-like or monopsonistic position and can lead to pricing policies unfavorable to the local economy. Multinational corporations may bring new technology and skills, but these are not always transferred effectively to the local workforce, and sometimes the technology is inappropriate to the factor proportions and the stage of sociological development of the local economy. Furthermore, multinationals sometime exhibit a bias toward sourcing their raw materials and manufactured input requirement from overseas, even when local sources are available or could be developed. This can have a negative side effect on local employment. Island governments need to be on the lookout for such effects. In addition, although some direct capital may flow in, in the longer run profits or income transfers flow out causing a drain on foreign exchange. Transfer pricing may be engaged in as well.

Considerable tax, tariff, and other concessions are often made by island governments to woo multinational companies, and frequently such companies play one island nation off against the other to obtain improved terms. This can be to the collective detriment of the group of island nations concerned. Other drawbacks of multinational corporations can include disregard for the environment and for local social structures and patterns and the possibilities of undue local political influences (cf., Tisdell, 1989b). But against this must be set a number of benefits. These can include transfer of more efficient technology, marketing and management skills, local supply of products that otherwise might not be supplied or supplied at higher cost if imported, and development and economic use of resources that otherwise might remain unexploited.

From the above, it is apparent that SINs have open economies from several points of view. They show a high degree of dependence on foreign trade (including in many cases trade in services, especially tourism), on foreign aid or private remittances from abroad, and on direct investment by multinational corporations in their modern sectors. Although many island microstates indicate that their goal is economic self-reliance, this seems to be an unrealistic goal for the smaller island states given their per capita income aspirations and their lack of genuine economic development possibilities. In many cases, real issues are being clouded both by aid donors' and by local nations' pretending that self-sustaining economic development is a real possibility in the near future for all small island microstates.

14

Some Final Reflections and Policy Perspectives

Speaking to one of the current authors, an economist concerned with the problems of Third World nations declared that the only significant issues for economists were to be found in the monetary sector. If that particular economist holds to his convictions, the reference to them in the present context should not disturb him, for he will probably never encounter it. The lack of space devoted to monetary matters in this volume should not be interpreted as an implicit statement of their unimportance. They simply did not fall within the intended scope of the current discussion. It is hoped that what has been included will contribute to the understanding of certain developmental issues facing SINs. Toward that understanding the present chapter summarizes what has been included while assessing the policy implications of that material.

STRUCTURAL AND EMPLOYMENT ISSUES

As was suggested very early in the present volume, some negative features have developed over the years in the relationships between developed nations and the jurisdictions that have collectively come to be called the Third World. These unfortunate matters are often reflected in the structures of various emerging economies. Very visible examples are frequently contained in the nature of Third World infrastructures, which due to external forces have taken on outward-looking configurations, which may not always support the general developmental goals of particular economies. In the case of small island economies, impressions obtained through the study or observation of larger Third World states may require some adjustment if they are to serve a useful purpose.

One of the major motivations behind the interest of developed nations in less fortunate parts of the world was the ongoing need for staple commodities. The international history of staple procurement shows little evidence that nations on the demand side of staples' markets designed staple enterprises with much regard for the needs of the supplier territories, many of which are now both independent and poor. In the case of SINs that have been involved in plantation agriculture or the supply of various other staples, infrastructures may or may not be conducive to more general developmental goals.

The utility of such infrastructures may be related to the size and geography of the jurisdictions in question. Very small island territories may be able to use staple-oriented infrastructures effectively for general development. Larger island economies may be suffering from problems related to outward-looking infrastructures. Regardless of the overall utility of such infrastructures, the ministates concerned will hardly be able to abandon them should staple exports become less central to their economies. As was suggested in Chapter 1, it is more probable that such territories will have to make do with such facilities and continue the variable costs related to their upkeep. Although minor adjustments can probably be undertaken, the overall costs of replacement may be prohibitive or, at the very least, may impact developmental priorities in an adverse fashion.

In the Caribbean region many small nations possess settlement patterns and domestic infrastructures dictated by plantation agriculture. In the South Pacific such configurations exist but are much less general. Current reliance upon staple exports by small island economies does not bode well for their development potential. Because the terms of trade are generally unfavorable to staple commodities, microstates relying upon such exports may be forced to initiate even more intensive staple production, even to the extent where such outputs take precedence over the supply of domestic food requirements.

In SINs, such as many in the Caribbean, the continuing demands of the trade in staples may even preclude the development of useful commerce within the region. In maximizing their contribution to world staple markets, the economies in question are actually competing among themselves.

It has been suggested that food imports in the Caribbean account for a large portion of the balance of payments difficulties being experienced in that region (Demas, 1988a, 160). On a policy level the alleviation of balance of payments pressures occasioned by food imports can perhaps be sought through interisland cooperation in production and intraregional exchange of foodstuffs (see Demas, 1988a). Such cooperation, and indeed any attempts at import substitution with respect to food products, will require removing an adequate amount of land resources from the production of staples for export. Government policy initiatives designed to diversify small island economies, which are too reliant upon staple exports, are to be recommended regardless of whether or not the staples in question are food items.

In the search for diversification, manufacturing, if feasible, may appear to be a seductive option. In recent years, firms or production units based in Third World nations have been quite successful in breaching world markets. In the case of SINs, geographical positioning may be a factor in their potential for success in manufacturing ventures aimed at external markets.

In the Caribbean region improvements in transportation and communications technology, not to mention proximity to North American markets, are assets with respect to the development of manufacturing for export. As was the case with primary activities, planners must consider the pressure manufacturing will place upon the infrastructure. Even on small islands where the infrastructure required by the secondary sector may serve domestic needs simultaneously, developmental priorities may have to be altered to secure the resources needed for infrastructure projects.

Planners must also pay special attention to foreign-owned manufacturing firms. One of the more serious issues in that regard, as referred to in Chapter 2, is "the global basis of decision making which results in the tendency inherent in direct investment from abroad to shift decision-making power in parts of the private sector outside the country" (Parry, 1973). The implication with respect to small island economies is not that hosting foreign-owned manufacturing facilities is always questionable but that such decisions should be examined on a case-by-case basis.

In seeking to attract corporate investors from abroad, policy makers in SINs should be careful with respect to requests for financial, environmental, or other concessions. As is the case with location decisions in metropolitan nations, specific islands will be attractive and/or suitable for certain firms irrespective of concessions. Concessions, if they are not cost free, may well reduce the advantages of hosting corporate facilities. The real or perceived need to offer concessions can be reduced or eliminated through cooperation between small island states that are potential competitors in attracting production facilities.

International firms may have various reasons for wanting to locate in small island economies. Among reasons deemed pertinent in the Caribbean region are availability of raw materials and low-cost labor, not to mention markets for the firms' products as well as for import-substituting industries controlled by those firms (Barry et al., 1984, 14).

Of course the potential for import substitution is a function of market size and, thus, in the case of small islands, provides still another reason for interisland cooperation.

In dealing with prospective corporate investors, planners in potential host territories must be realistic about what their location has to offer. In the Caribbean region, as mentioned above, proximity to major markets is important, but beyond that various islands offer low-cost literate labor, political and financial stability, and dependable legal systems. What the planners hope to gain includes jobs and needed foreign exchange. With respect to the latter consideration, the local content of exports, the final disposition of profits earned, and the needs of the corporations for imports are important. Reaching a broad understanding of the concerns in this paragraph as they pertain to contemplated hostings should be an advanced goal of the planning authorities. Such planning should reduce potential problems while improving opportunities for benefits.

Small island planners should be selective in accepting corporate projects and should choose those presumed to have continuing positive potential in the international economy. Once again the planners must exhibit realism in appraising their nations' potential as export platforms. Granting various concessions may be unnecessary and even counterproductive. Firms making decisions based upon such concessions may prove to be undesirable. Competition between small island economies through concessionary practices is generally undesirable. If the indigenous planners are prudent regarding the matters indicated here, it is hoped that their potential for success with the manufacturing facilities that do locate within their jurisdictions will be improved.

Any discussion of the development potential in various economic activities in SINs must include services. Those services induced by demand generated from income earned from staples or manufacturing are hardly central to developmental processes. All the same, various services for profit are far from inconsequential, especially in island economies with urban centers. Such services cover a wide range of activities, including retailing and distribution, tourist-related businesses, transport, finance, insurance, and real estate, as well as legal, accounting, and other business services, not to mention health-related services.

Improvements in transportation and communications have made it much simpler to acquire services from distant suppliers (Feketekuty, 1988, 8). This in itself makes it at least theoretically possible for small island economies to participate in such service pursuits. If various business services have actually become facilitators of change in the world economy, undoubtedly those activities should be examined in the search for major service roles in small island economies. However, even menial service pursuits may benefit those near the base of the income pyramid in Third World settings.

Production facilities themselves owe their success in small island settings to an array of sophisticated services operating in the world economy. Feketekuty has suggested that international business would not be possible without an extensive international trade in services (1988, 18). He explains that the services in question include, besides transportation and communications, finance and insurance, "the know-how, and all the other support systems that are needed for world commerce" (1988, 18). Despite the obvious logic in such pronouncements, it is not obvious that many of the services referred to will actually locate in small island settings. In cases where the facilitating services are themselves multinational firms, it may be more likely that they will boast branches in Third World jurisdictions (McKee, 1988, 118).

Certainly the potential benefits of hosting such activities in the Caribbean region are known. Demas has called for the production of such services for export (1988b, 14). Among the services he considered were engineering and construction, petroleum and bauxite technology, higher education, and agronomy. He felt that such services could be sold to other Third World nations. Developed nations were also included as potential customers for offshore university education, health, finance, and information processing (1988b, 14).

The availability of processing and communications equipment varies widely throughout the Caribbean. Many smaller jurisdictions have little to offer, and it is not obvious that the installation of such equipment would draw much business toward them. In the Caribbean region transportation and communications and actual location have a major effect upon the potential for supplying international services. Because of this, the developmental potential from such service groups is clearly destination specific. In the Caribbean region some jurisdictions are marketing specific services to the developed world. Combinations of such service groups have emerged as leading sectors in various Caribbean territories.

Perhaps the most obvious of these service subgroups has been activities related to tourism. Beyond that, however, various Caribbean jurisdictions have emerged as financial centers active in the international economy. The driving force behind the emergence of financial centers appears to be the need for various multinational enterprises to distance themselves from certain government rules and regulations. Whether the activities of such centers have positive effects upon the host economies is not always clear. Certainly they generate a demand for many auxiliary business and accounting services, not to mention legal and trust expertise. Thus it would appear that they generate professional and semiprofessional employment opportunities for local residents.

That certain economies are already quite successful in offshore banking circles may make it much more difficult for would-be financial centers to replicate their success. Certainly an unlimited number of centers in the same region cannot be expected to succeed by competing in the same activity.

Services facilitating the location of manufacturing activity in small island economies may make a positive contribution to development. Also those facilitating operations in the international economy may set the direction of some small island economies. Whether they can constitute a general solution to developmental needs in the islands concerned is doubtful.

In many small Third World nations, the public sector of the economy is proportionally larger in terms of its share of the labor force than is the case in more developed economies. This may mean that the government sector is less efficient than its counterparts in developed nations. It may also mean that the ranks of government workers are overextended as a means of creating jobs. In spite of this relative overextension, some small states may not be able to supply the quality and range of public services prevalent in the developed world.

Some small Pacific island states are heavily dependent on foreign aid to assist in the costs of government. That practice is less prevalent in the Caribbean. In jurisdictions that rely on foreign aid, long-range planning on the part of public agencies may be difficult because the aid may be somewhat unpredictable. Any drop in aid may force cuts in government employment, which in turn will translate immediately into more general economic difficulties for the jurisdiction concerned.

In general a major impact of the public sector in small island economies has been to foster urbanization and economic centralization. The mere location of government agencies fosters this phenomenon. Induced spending from government activity further strengthens the trend toward urban concentration. As an urban area expands on its government base, it becomes attractive to potential in-migrants because of the greater availability of public services within its confines. In some small islands the economy can come close to a city-state configuration. In such jurisdictions this is not necessarily a negative externality. However, too much emphasis on central government functions in the case of archipelagic nations can work to the detriment of rural areas and more remote settlements. All small island economies should be careful not to allow the strength of the government to cause a permanent overemphasis to the detriment of private development potential.

In some SINs tourism has become so central to the economy that it overshadows most other activities. In many Third World jurisdictions, tourism has emerged with little preplanning with respect to its potential impact upon overall developmental objectives. This is true even though it was generally perceived as an activity that would promote employment opportunities while earning needed foreign exchange.

Small island states in the Caribbean, the Pacific, and the Indian Ocean are encouraging the industry as a vehicle for economic growth. Despite widespread and enthusiastic acceptance, the industry is far from a panacea. Its abilities to increase income and employment are often limited. It can have adverse impacts upon income distribution as well as the balance of payments. Among small economies it can be an unstable source of foreign income and can undermine traditional industries. In addition it can generate negative environmental and social externalities. Thus, small states considering the industry should at least tread carefully.

Tourism can cause small economies to become even more dependent upon imports. The needs of the visitors contribute to this. With respect to food, tourist tastes generate imports, which may create a demonstration effect among local residents. This in turn may impact local food production and in some cases the prospects of rural development. Tourism may also increase urban pressure because of the location of facilities and resorts in and around existing urban areas. This is especially true of mass-marketed types of tourism whereas more sophisticated segments of the industry may search out less crowded locations — a proposition deserving planners' attention.

The urban pressure exerted by tourism is hardly surprising. Visitors may require facilities that are available only in urban environments, such as shopping and medical services, not to mention external communications linkages and cultural options. From the point of view of operators of tourist facilities, urban environments hold certain advantages as well, not the least of which may be easy access to labor pools. Thus an urban bias in the tourist industry is hardly surprising.

One of the major incentives for encouraging tourism in Third World settings is that it is often considered labor intensive. Oddly enough this perception may be oversimplification, because the capital requirements of the industry are extensive. In addition many positions in the tourist industry may be filled by foreigners. Often managers, accountants, head chefs, and other relatively skilled personnel are in short supply within domestic labor pools. Some personnel are required to have linguistic skills, not to mention a knowledge of foreign customs. As a consequence the main pool of positions available to local residents may be of the unskilled variety. Added to difficulties referred to here is the seasonality of the industry in some locations. Depending upon the local demand for seasonal versus year-round employment, this may be a problem.

Tourism may exclude local residents from areas set aside for foreign visitors. If such exclusions include areas used by the local poor for food gathering, the plight of that segment of the population will worsen. In the same vein, demand by visitors for local food stocks may raise the prices of such commodities. This may be a special problem in small island states not well endowed with natural resources (e.g., agricultural land and/or fisheries). In some areas visitors demand local products for which the local market is modest or nonexistent. Such circumstances must be included in the overall appraisal of the industry's utility in specific jurisdictions.

Although tourism is a growth industry throughout the world, it is not without risk to specific jurisdictions because it relies on a foreign clientele. Coupled with that reality is the fact that tourist facilities are not readily transferrable to other pursuits. Thus, a drop in demand will result in large sunk costs. Even the sought after balance of payments surpluses are not necessarily risk free. Where such ends are realized, they may cause adverse adjustments in exchange rates, thus disadvantaging established export sectors.

Tourism can also have adverse environmental impacts. Buildings and support infrastructure, including transportation facilities, not to mention water and sewage requirements, may all contribute to this problem. If environmental damage is severe, it may even deter tourists. Thus it may be advantageous for certain island states to limit the quantity of tourists in the interest of maintaining a predictable flow of customers for the future. Such limitations would protect social and cultural environments as well.

Thus, SINs should use a certain amount of caution in pursuing development through tourism. If kept in sensible proportions, with respect to other developmental needs of potential host nations, it can be beneficial. However, where the industry is relied upon exclusively as a vehicle for development, the risks appear to be magnified, especially in very small economies.

DEMOGRAPHIC AND SOCIOECONOMIC ISSUES

No discussion of the developmental problems of small island economies would be complete without including the phenomenon of urbanization. The problems these small nations are experiencing in that regard are similar in nature if not in extent to those of larger Third World jurisdictions. Some SINs may become little more than city-states. In such jurisdictions the shift of the economy away from agriculture toward secondary and tertiary pursuits may cause more impetus for urbanization than has been documented in larger emerging nations.

Certainly urban development in SINs is hardly a microcosm of the experience of larger nations. In many such states the principal urban center owes its existence to governmental functions, often dating to colonial times. From the outset the urban centers were major fulcrums of power. It is hardly surprising if they have been further strengthened as the economies that housed them grew. Today the urban centers in some island economies have become the preserve of sophisticated arrays of service activities geared to the international economy. Those services, coupled with continuing governmental roles, give such centers impacts upon their national economies proportionally much greater than those in major urban centers in larger Third World economies. In the current volume experience in Barbados and the Bahamas has been cited as evidence of the phenomenon described above.

In an urban setting among SINs, the labor absorption problem revolves around the needs of the service sector. Certain services, notably transportation and communications and aspects of tourism, may have little employment to offer island residents, relying instead upon imported labor. The policy implications of this situation seem clear. For particular economies to gain maximum benefit from the services described, local workers must be given access to jobs related to them. Whether this means on-the-job training or specialized educational experiences, the nations concerned must take appropriate steps if they are to gain maximum domestic benefits from a sophisticated urban service sector.

Where domestic job access and upward labor mobility can be encouraged, certain small island economies can make progress by relying on an urbanized externally oriented service sector. The success of the Bahamas and, perhaps, Barbados supports that contention. However entry to the ranks of viable international service centers is constrained by demand from beyond the shores of aspiring island economies. Certainly unlimited opportunities do not exist for the emergence of externally oriented urban economies among SINs.

In some larger SINs urban development more in line with that experienced by larger Third World nations may be more likely. In Jamaica, for example, Kingston appears to be a smaller version of the Third World metropolitan prototype. Clearly the development potential of

SINs in an urban mode differs depending upon whether they can emerge as modern city-states or are constrained by patterns exhibited by larger emerging nations. In the latter mode they will experience problems relating to critical mass, whereas the city-state configuration may offer promise to some jurisdictions.

In the case of archipelago states, emphasis upon a capital city puts pressure on that location and may cause population movements, resulting in uneven opportunities in areas far removed from the capital. In the Caribbean, the Bahamas are an example of this phenomenon. In the Pacific, the Marshall Islands, Kiribati, and Tuvalu fit the same pattern. Overurbanization on their principal atolls has caused problems of overcrowding, poor housing, rising pollution, and crime, not to mention social disorganization.

Urbanization seems to be playing a major role in shaping development patterns in SINs. In the Caribbean this has been characterized in some cases by sophisticated service linkages to the world economy. In the South Pacific urban expansion seems to be more dependent upon civil service employment. In both areas urban growth appears destined to continue and with it an expansion in service dependence.

Beyond the problems of urbanization in small island economies, more general population issues have emerged. Many such states are too small to establish domestic markets of a size needed to ensure economic development. At the same time rising populations are taxing food and other resources, thus making the economies in question more dependent upon external linkages. The islands of the Caribbean, for example, have been experiencing severe, ongoing population pressures. The method of coping with population pressure has generally been out migration. The position in the Pacific is more or less similar.

In very small island economies, urban survival options are not plentiful for those trapped in rural surplus labor pools. In the face of this, the stage might seem set for such population surpluses to emigrate. Although population surpluses do originate in rural areas, those surpluses with the possible exception of the Haitian case, do not appear to be the source of continuing emigration patterns among the small nations of the Caribbean region. Instead the Caribbean states have been losing migrants that have more education, better health, and higher earning capacities than their typical countrymen (Pastor, 1985, 14).

Thus when skilled workers leave the country, their actions have very little to do with the traditional patterns of surplus labor so evident in the general development literature. Because of this, their leaving may hardly contribute to domestic labor absorption but rather will open job skill gaps that may prove difficult to bridge. Thus emigration and internal population movements involve different population groups and have very different impacts upon developmental processes.

Despite emigration the ministates in question must still find ways to employ their surplus labor. In the Caribbean those in surplus labor pools may find themselves illegal aliens, should they elect to leave their homelands. The movement of such persons may complicate the labor situation in their elected destinations. On a personal level such migrants may find themselves exploited in their new homes. On the part of potential destination states, draconian travel regulations may emerge aimed at keeping out unwanted surplus population. Such measures may in turn impede normal interisland relations, thus perhaps interfering with developmental processes.

In the case of unskilled surplus labor, the purpose behind interisland movement may be mere survival. Such migration will continue as long as it ensures subsistence. In the face of such movements, the wages of unskilled workers in recipient territories will be depressed.

In the modern world migration does not appear to be a feasible strategy of population control for SINs. A new stringency with respect to the acceptance of migrants on the part of developed nations ensures that those who are admitted will possess employable skills. Even the alleviation of population pressure through temporary migration may have doubtful validity if the temporary migrants are skilled workers. In that instance source nations are unable to reap the benefits of their investment in training and education.

If SINs hope to improve their lot, more economic cooperation between them will be required, especially with respect to training and placing labor. Growth in their respective economies ultimately would relieve their surplus labor problems. Attention to actual growth strategies would appear to be more directly capable of eliciting material progress than does relying on exporting surplus population.

Few would argue against the need for education in any scenario designed to encourage development. However, education, if necessary to development, is hardly sufficient to effect it. The idea that education will solve labor absorption problems in Third World nations is undoubtedly borrowed from experiences or perceptions related to advanced nations. The development of realistic educational policies in the Third World will require major alterations in preconceptions. These adjustments may be especially pertinent to the needs of small island economies.

Educational investment and economic growth are directly related, but the identity of the causal partner may be masked in some cases. The returns to educational investment are dependent on the availability of suitable complementary resources and economic opportunities for those who become educated. In jurisdictions where the complementary factors are limited, as may be the case in various SINs, the paybacks from educational investments may be low.

Educational requirements can be used as screening devices, which may help in selecting specific types of individuals for certain tasks. If the system is heavily subsidized by government, there may be overinvestment in the sorting procedures, and their costs may exceed the marginal benefits to society. SINs with limited funds would do well to avoid such overinvestment. The danger of excess expenditure is increased if such jurisdictions attempt simply to replicate educational systems found in developed countries.

In many developing nations, including many South Pacific island states, educational subsidies rise with the level of education. This is thought to support the haves over the have nots. Many feel that greater participation in education, among other things, can help reduce income inequality. In the Caribbean no evidence has suggested that improvements in education have lessened the surplus labor problem. In the Pacific islands rising levels of education have been paralleled by rising unemployment rates, especially among the young.

Nations hoping to develop presumably require certain types of skilled labor. If educational resources are adjusted to supply those skills, a by-product of the process is that those acquiring such training may be able to enter international labor markets. This phenomenon is not what is commonly referred to as the brain drain although it is related. The brain drain as it pertains to small island economies has to do with the loss of professionally trained personnel to foreign labor markets.

Although the brain drain has received considerable media exposure, in and of itself it may not be as damaging to SINs as initial perceptions may indicate. As mentioned earlier (Chapter 8), "Expatriate nuclear engineers from small island nations are not depriving those jurisdictions of a nuclear power industry." That particular industry may not be needed. The main loss to small island economies occasioned by expatriate professionals is not the specific skills of particular individuals but the tasks those individuals could have accomplished had they not emigrated — tasks that may even have required different training.

In SINs with population or surplus labor problems, the out migration of trained workers may even be a positive influence. In some nations education can even aid in controlling population pressures by providing individuals with skills that are salable elsewhere, provided, of course, that the skills in question are not needed at home. Thus, it may not be surprising if certain governments pay little more than lip service to the brain drain and related issues. In some cases the lack of concern may be further strengthened by the role that remittances play.

Nevertheless, the international market for professional personnel may have further implications for the SINs in question. The credentialing processes in international labor markets may require training inappropriate to the home market. International licensing often produces health professionals equipped to deal with the needs of the developed world rather than those of the nations from which they emigrated.

In the case of small island economies, the implications of the brain drain and general educational considerations are intertwined. Educational systems in such nations must reflect local needs, which may vary from island to island. Plantation economies will have very different educational needs from those based on tourism. Vocational education would benefit most small island states. In the South Pacific the school system could benefit from adjustments toward vocational education. Among SINs too many educational processes are in tune with the needs of developed nations, not the SINs. In some cases this is a legacy from colonial experiences. Yet in certain areas of the Caribbean, the growth of literate, unemployed labor pools may be simply a product of rapidly expanding populations.

In SINs with university facilities, the needs of the domestic economy can be targeted in educational processes. Such higher educational facilities can even be geared to broader regional needs. Certainly sound policy requires that all levels of education be geared to delivering needed human capital. If such forms of capital are not being supplied, educational adjustments are indicated.

One of the negative overspills from socioeconomic development, coupled with urbanization and industrialization, has been a rising crime rate (de Albuquerque, 1984, 94). This being so, policy makers in SINs are faced with the need to add costly law enforcement programs to already overburdened priority lists. These new programs may actually be competing with developmental programs for public funds.

Rather than total eradication, economists and other social scientists agree that the practical policy goal with respect to crime in most societies is to keep it within acceptable bounds. That being the case, Third World nations may rationally allow higher levels of criminal activity than are tolerated in developed nations. That policy may dictate establishing pecking orders of criminal activities to be eliminated, reduced, or tolerated. As in most societies crimes against persons will probably head most lists, followed by property crimes. In smaller and poorer nations, the costs of the criminal justice infrastructure may take a very large part of public funds and may force policy makers to ignore so-called victimless crimes.

In some cases activities regarded as criminal in the developed world may even seem to be making positive contributions to Third World economies. The drug trade may fall into this category. The continuing strength of the international drug market may seem tempting to economies faced with the vagaries of demand or other staples. The employment the industry generates and its ability to earn foreign exchange may be persuasive. As long as drugs — if manufactured domestically — are exported, the industry may be placed in the category of victimless crimes. The same casting may occur in small islands that serve as transshipment centers. Unfortunately with respect to drugs, production for export and transshipment lock those involved into permanent association with the international drug industry.

The location of criminal activities is affected by the proximity and extent of markets as well as by competition from other countries. The Caribbean islands are well placed with respect to markets on the North American mainland but may face competition in some respects from Latin American nations. The small island economies of the South Pacific are more isolated, and the criminal activity faced by them appears to be on a smaller scale from what prevails in various Caribbean nations.

Victimless crimes, which appear to be prevalent among SINs, do not stop at the international drug trade. Various forms of international financial manipulations may also be seen to be victimless in the domestic sense. This activity may include parking funds, money laundering, tax evasion, capital flight, and various forms of securities, investment, and real estate fraud. Success in these operations requires state-of-the-art transportation and communications linkages, political stability, and a sound financial system committed to bank secrecy.

Although some of the activities referred to above may occur in various well-established offshore banking centers, they may be a distinct threat to various other jurisdictions hoping to use offshore banking as a development strategy. Quite possibly those centers will attract questionable activities as international pressure pushes those practices out of established centers. Thus, the list of potential customers for fledgling financial centers may include drug traffickers, gun runners, and other participants in various forms of organized and nonorganized criminal activities (Walter, 1985, 3). Once again the policy makers in such jurisdictions may view the activities cited as victimless in a domestic sense. Where this occurs, permanent linkages may be established between the small economies involved and the international criminal underworld.

The activities discussed above deserve careful consideration from anyone concerned with the fortunes of SINs. Involvement with the international drug trade together with questionable international financial machinations may seem to be relatively benign on the domestic front. Such activities provide a certain amount of employment and may help with foreign exchange. Thus, they are given from low to zero attention by enforcement officials and, indeed, may even be supported by otherwise respectable governments.

Small island economies may be particularly susceptible to such international activities. The unfortunate involvements accompanying the activities may lead to corruption of public officials as well as to expansion of indigenous crime. Drugs, for example, may leach into the local population, causing increases in crimes against persons and property. In SINs, such circumstances can interfere with other developmental options.

One of the activities that crime will impact is tourism. Some crime against tourists seems inevitable in Third World jurisdictions. However, when such offenses reach a critical mass, the resulting adverse publicity will slow the flow of visitors. Small island economies that have opted for heavy involvement with tourism are at special risk. In locations where tourism is seasonal, witness many Caribbean economies, the off-season may see an increase of crimes against local residents.

It would appear that certain crimes, which may have been perceived to be victimless in a domestic sense, deserve special attention by policy makers in SINs. Although viewed on the surface as relatively benign, they may have a greater potential for permanent economic damage than more violent and, thus, more obvious crimes against people.

ENVIRONMENTAL AND NATURAL RESOURCE ISSUES

As was noted in Chapter 10, the degree of agricultural dependence varies considerably among small island economies. In both the Caribbean and the Pacific, many such jurisdictions rely heavily upon some form of primary exports. Some of the risks in this practice have already been noted. In addition, with respect to agriculture, natural disasters such as hurricanes or cyclones can affect supplies, and many of the economies of the regions being discussed are at considerable risk in that regard. Crops may also be at risk from accidentally introduced pests and diseases. Thus, it would appear that export-oriented agriculture may be an even less dependable base for development than was suggested in the more general discussion of primary products (Chapter 1).

Compared to the Caribbean a good deal of agricultural activity among the islands of the Pacific is of the subsistence variety. Although some plantations do exist, in Fiji, for example, the pattern in commercial agriculture is small holdings. The wisdom of abandoning subsistence agriculture in favor of the commercial variety is a debatable point, both with respect to Pacific locations and those in the Caribbean with subsistence holdings. Several uncertainties pertaining to commercial agriculture as an export sector have been referred to above. Beyond those, agricultural exports can lock the economies in question into dependence on more developed economies. Commercialization will also contribute to the destruction of traditional social structures, a consideration concerning the Pacific islands much more than those in the Caribbean.

By and large, policy makers in island jurisdictions have favored commercialization. Whether or not for that reason, subsistence agriculture is declining in SINs. Accompanying that decline has been a reduction in the variety of planted species and an increased dependence on foreign foods. In some cases rising food imports have been responsible for reducing the regularity of food consumption where cash flows are variable.

The reduction of food imports would appear to be an important goal for many small island economies. Such a course, accomplished by import substitution in the agricultural sector, would improve nutrition while putting people to work and easing an unnecessary foreign exchange burden. An emphasis on supplying food needs domestically may mean adjustments in agricultural methods and even firm size. If accomplished successfully, it would ease the developmental burden on urban-based sectors and perhaps reduce certain unwanted pressures inherent in the expansion of urban populations.

As Demas (1988a, 1963) has suggested with respect to the Caribbean, an especially attractive policy would be import replacement, where foreign foods are replaced by indigenous products rather than locally grown foreign foods. Despite the logic of what Demas has suggested, island economies may find barriers in the way of any food-related import substitution. Among such obstacles may be official indifference (Crusol, 1980, 122). Crusol also referred to the inflexibility of the plantation system and the sometimes dependent relationship between large estates and small farms as well as a taste for imports and the external slant of island business (1980, 122 ff.).

Plantations, where they exist, tend to be somewhat more efficient than smaller holdings. However, most are involved in monoculture and use artificial fertilizers and pesticides. Thus, their operations can cause ecological difficulties. Plantations appear to be able to achieve greater weed control, sometimes at the expense of greater soil erosion. Thus, the need for economic efficiency in agriculture does not necessarily lend total support to the encouragement of plantations. Efficiency gains to the economy through plantation agriculture may be counterbalanced by an inflexibly uneven income distribution. Plantation profits, regardless of ownership, may be invested abroad. If plantations generate dualism, they may actually interfere with developmental objectives. Planners in economies with a strong plantation base may be well advised to encourage more diverse developmental configurations. Agriculture hardly appears to be a sufficient base for sustained development.

Despite the fact that many small island economies are not noted for their resource endowments, the output of such nations tends to be natural resource intensive. The island economies of the South Pacific control vast reaches of ocean. Although the areas in question have low productivity of biomass per unit area, fish production is large because of the size of the areas involved. The small nations concerned hardly have the wherewithal to assert effective control of their rights.

The principal fishery resource involved in the central and South Pacific is tuna. Most developing island nations cannot exploit this resource directly. Most island populations have little experience or expertise in offshore fisheries and little desire to spend the time at sea required to exploit such a resource. Capital costs, lack of access to overseas markets, and lack of management skills also impede the direct and effective participation of island residents in offshore, commercial fisheries.

Some islands may gain some benefit by collecting resource rents from foreign interests (Waugh, 1986). However, foreign operations provide no jobs for island residents and have little other positive influence beyond the fees paid. In addition the island economies have no way to monitor the size of catches or the impact that the fishing operations have on marine life in general. From a developmental point of view, the utility of the involvement of specific islands with foreign fishing interests, abstracting from environmental considerations, revolves around the use of the rents received. On the surface, fish processing plants operated as joint ventures in the territories concerned may be beneficial in that they provide employment. However, if such ventures employ foreign managers, they may cause problems similar to what can occur in manufacturing facilities (See Chapter 2).

In the Caribbean, fishing does not play a major role. Some jurisdictions actually import fish. Where possible, it would appear that such practices should be curtailed in favor of local varieties. However, the implementation of that suggestion may be difficult in the face of long-standing customs and tastes. It would appear as though more attention to commercial fishing throughout the Caribbean region would have very positive results, both nutritionally and in economic terms through increases in employment and a lessened need for food imports.

Although forests are not a major resource in many small island states, timber has been an important export in various larger island nations in the Pacific. In the South Pacific foreign interests have dominated the industry. Such interests are contributing to the disappearance of rain forests and species dependent upon them. In cases where unprocessed logs are exported, the industry does not realize its local employment potential. Cutover areas may be subject to erosion. Forestry involving selective cutting and replanting may be a useful industry in small island settings even though timber, because of its bulk, may not be a competitive product when shipped over long distances. The Caribbean region could probably benefit from reforestation in some cases, but it is doubtful if the timber industry will even be a major factor in that region.

Foreign interests have been able to place resource-related commercial ventures in Third World settings with relative ease. The danger in such activities is their potential for inflicting permanent environmental damage. Such operations may also be less than sympathetic to their impact on local populations. In many SINs commercial fishing, forestry, and mining are heavily dependent upon direct foreign investment. The output of such ventures is intended for external markets and, thus, subject to the uncertainties discussed in Chapter 1. It would appear that such an industry often will not provide a continuing and predictable contribution to the development of host jurisdictions. This being the case, SINs should not be too anxious to overextend themselves to such activities.

SINs are quite dependent upon living resources. In many cases harm to these resources translates into reduced incomes for island residents and may increase the flow of migrants to more developed nations. Other impacts may include increased prices in world markets if the harm has reduced supplies of exported resource products. In cases where the resources in question were a tourist attraction, additional economic losses may occur. Resource damage can have multifaceted impacts, some of which reach well beyond the boundaries of the small islands.

Another matter of environmental concern is the impact that the greenhouse effect may have. Even moderate rises in the sea level will have a disastrous impact upon many small islands. It has been estimated that a one-meter rise in the sea level would render many atolls uninhabitable in their present form (Crocombe, 1981, 1). Even rather small increases will cause erosion and salinization problems.

In the Pacific nuclear contamination has been an issue. Such jurisdictions can do little in the face of ongoing testing because they rely on foreign aid and are militarily weak (Herrman, 1989, 56). Another type of environmental encroachment of concern to many small islands is the dumping of toxic wastes in ocean areas close to them, not to mention the possibility of such wastes actually being dumped on their land. Islands near major shipping routes are also at risk from oil spills. Fishing techniques that sweep deepwater areas clean of life are another concern. Developed countries can also impact island environments through resource demands, the location of dirty manufacturing facilities, and environmentally destructive forms of tourism.

High on the list of domestic risks to island environments is population pressure. This can lead to more than optimal levels of land clearing, overharvesting of inshore fisheries, and excessive urbanization. Natural resources in the vicinity of urban centers are often depleted or destroyed by wastes. Human wastes from urban areas can cause health problems. Even the ocean disposal of sewage may not be environmentally sound because of impacts upon coral and various other living resources.

Many island states suffer from water shortages. Low islands in the Pacific rely heavily on rainwater, collected in tanks, and on wells. Higher islands mostly rely upon running water for drinking and supplement their overall needs by rainwater collection. In economies where water is in short supply, pollution through the use of agrochemicals and through waste disposal is a serious risk. In jurisdictions where water supplies are in such precarious balance, policy makers should pay special attention to selecting or encouraging commercial activities that do not further complicate an already serious situation.

Wildlife is at serious risk in most of the small island environments in question. Loss of habitat for various reasons, coupled with invasions of exotic wildlife, including feral animals, have interfered drastically with native species. On the policy level, setting aside protected areas may not always be feasible, but measures should be considered to eradicate or control unwanted introduced species and to protect endangered species from them.

Some environmental problems are of natural origin. Many island states are located where natural disasters are possible. Where these occur, the jurisdictions in question may require foreign assistance. Besides hurricanes and cyclones, periodic droughts and fires occur (Connell, 1988, 36). Health problems are also an issue in some states. Malaria, some strains of which have become drug resistant, is an example (Simms, 1989). Hazards such as those referred to here can certainly interfere with developmental efforts. Thus, it would appear that policy makers should give high priority to environmental matters in their developmental plans.

Matters relating to the environment and natural resources have an international dimension. In some cases they demonstrate just how dependent SINs are on matters beyond their shores. Although international considerations have been addressed in Chapter 13, a final word is still in order concerning the openness of the economies in question. As can be seen throughout this volume, size has conspired to deny many SINs the degree of economic sovereignty taken for granted in larger nations. Even larger Third World nations can hope to increase control over their own economies if they are successful in their developmental objectives. In the case of many SINs, import substitution may never be feasible on a scale sufficient to allay ongoing demands on foreign exchange, which will limit the independence of their economies. Many SINs may experience ongoing needs for foreign aid, not to mention foreign direct investment. Even remittances signal a needed continuing link to the outside world in some of the smaller SINs. Thus, the nations in question must go about the process of development in a climate where international considerations are ever present and where they may even be constrained by those considerations in their domestic adjustment policies.

Selected Bibliography

Abbott, George C. (1974). "Estimates of the Growth of the Population of the West Indies to 1975," *Social and Economic Studies,* Vol. 23, pp. 242–43.

Abdula, Norma (1977). "The Labor Force in the Commonwealth Caribbean: A Statistical Analysis." St. Augustine, Trinidad: Institute of Social and Economic Research, University of the West Indies, Occasional Papers on Human Resources, No. 1, June.,

Ahluwalia, M. S. (1976). "Inequality, Poverty and Development." *Journal of Public Economics,* Vol. 3, pp. 307–42.

Ahmed, S. A. (1987). "Perceptions of Socio-Economic and Cultural Impact of Tourism in Sri Lanka — A Research Study." *Marga,* Vol. 8, No. 4, pp. 34–63.

Anderson, R. W. (1976). *The Economics of Crime.* London: Macmillan.

Anon (1986). *Distance Education.* Manila: Asian Development Bank.

Anon (1989). "Forum Slams Wall of Death." *Pacific Islands Monthly,* June, p. 31.

Arrow, K. (1973). "Higher Education as a Filter." *Journal of Public Economics,* Vol. 2, pp. 143–216.

Baksh, I. J. (1984). "Factors Influencing Occupational Expectations of Secondary School Students in Trinidad and Tobago." *Social and Economic Studies,* Vol. 33, No. 3, pp. 1–29.

Barry, T., et al. (1984). *The Other Side of Paradise: Foreign Control in the Caribbean.* New York: Grove Press.

Becker, G. S. (1975). *Human Capital,* 2nd ed. New York: Columbia University Press.

Beckford, George L. (1972). *Persistent Poverty: Underdevelopment in Plantation Economies of the Third World.* London: Oxford University Press (reprinted in abbreviated form, Morant Bay, Jamaica: Maroon, 1983).

171

Beckford, George L., and Norman Girvan (eds.) (1989). *Development in Suspense.* Kingston: Friedrich Ebert Stiftung.

Beenstock, M. (1979). "Corruption and Development." *World Development,* Vol. 7, No. 1, January, pp. 15–24.

Behrman, J. R., and B. L. Wolfe (1984). "The Socioeconomic Impact of Schooling in a Developing Country." *Review of Economics and Statistics,* Vol. 66, No. 2, pp. 296–303.

Belassa, Bela (1983). "Structural Adjustment Policies in Developing Economies." *World Development,* Vol. 10, No. 1, January, pp. 23–38.

Bertram, I. G. (1986). "Sustainable Development in Pacific Micro-Economies." *World Development,* Vol. 14, No. 7, pp. 809–992.

Bertram, I. B., and R. F. Watters (1985). "The MIRAB Economy in South Pacific Microstates." *Pacific Viewpoint,* Vol. 26, No. 3, pp. 497–519.

____. (1986). "The MIRAB Process: Earlier Analyses in Context." *Pacific Viewpoint,* Vol. 27, pp. 47–59.

Blaug, M. (1976). "Human Capital Theory: A Slightly Jaundiced Survey." *Journal of Economic Literature,* Vol. 14, pp. 827–55.

Bloomquist, A. G. (1986). "Higher Education and the Markets for Educated Labour in LDC's: Theoretical Approaches and Implications." *Pakistan Development Review,* Vol. 25, No. 3, pp. 249–73.

Braithwaite, John (1979). *Inequality, Crime and Public Policy.* London: Rutledge and Kegan Paul, 1979.

Brana-Shute, Rosemary and Gary (eds.) (1980). *Crime in the Caribbean.* Gainesville: University of Florida Press.

Brock, Colin (ed.) (1986). *The Caribbean in Europe: Aspects of the West Indian Experience in Britain, France, and the Netherlands.* London: Frank Cass.

Brookfield, M., and R. G. Ward (1988). *New Directions in the South Pacific.* Canberra, Australia: Academy of Social Sciences.

Browne, Christopher (with Douglas A. Scott) (1989). *Economic Development in Seven Pacific Islands.* Washington, D.C.: International Monetary Fund.

Buffermayer, Jay Ralph (1970). *Emigration of High-Level Manpower and National Development: A Case Study of Jamaica.* Ph.D. dissertation, University of Pittsburgh.

Buterworth, Douglas, and John K. Chance (1981). *Latin American Urbanization.* New York: Cambridge University Press.

Candilis, Wray O. (ed.) (1988). *United States Service Industries Handbook.* New York: Praeger.

Chernick, Sidney E. (1978). *The Commonwealth Caribbean: The Integration Experience.* Report of a mission sent to the Commonwealth Caribbean by the World Bank. Baltimore: The Johns Hopkins University Press.

Chiswick, C. U. (1984). "The Impact of Education Policy on Economic Development: Quantity, Quality, and Earnings of Labor." *Economic Education Review,* Vol. 3, No. 2, pp. 121–30.

Clark, C. G. (1971). "Population Problems in the Caribbean." *Revista Geographica,* Vol. 75, pp. 31–48.

Clinard, M. B. (1976). "The Problem of Crime and Its Control in Developing Countries." In D. Biles (ed.). *Crime in Papua New Guinea.* Canberra: Australian Institute of Criminology.

Clinard, M. B., and D. J. Abbot. (1973). *Crime in Developing Coutnries: A Comparative Perspective.* New York: John Wiley.

Cohen, Stephen S., and John Zysman (1987). *Manufacturing Matters.* New York: Basic Books.

Connell, J. (1988). *Sovereignty and Survival, Island Microstates in the Third World.* Research Monograph No. 3, Department of Geography, University of Sydney.

____. (1986). "Population, Migration, and Problems of Atoll Development in the South Pacific." *Pacific Studies,* Vol. 9, No. 2, pp. 41–58.

Conroy. J. D. (1982). *Essays on the Development Experience in Papua New Guinea.* Port Moresby: Institute of Applied Social and Economic Research.

Copland, J. W., and T. S. Lucas (eds.) (1988). *Giant Clams in Asia and the Pacific.* Canberra: Australian Centre for International Agricultural Research.

Crocombe, R. (1989). "Some Problems Facing Pacific Islands Countries." *Pacific Perspective,* Vol. 14, No. 1, pp. 1–7.

Cross, Malcolm (1979). *Urbanization and Urban Growth in the Caribbean.* London: Cambridge University Press.

Crusol, Jean (1980). *Economies insulaires de la Caraibe: Aspects theoriques et pratiques du developpement.* Paris: Editions Caribeennes.

Dann, Graham (1984). *The Quality of Life in Barbados.* London: MacMillan.

David, R. (1988). "Marshall Islands. No Rainbow for Nuclear Refugees." *Pacific Islands Monthly,* August, p. 14.

Davison, R. B. (1962). *West Indian Migrants: Social and Economic Facts from the West Indies.* London: Oxford University Press.

de Albuquerque, K. (1984). "A Comparative Analysis of Violent Crime in the Caribbean." *Social and Economic Studies,* Vol. 33, No. 3, September, pp. 93–143.

de Kadt, E. (1979). *Tourism — Passport to Development.* New York: Oxford University Press.

Delimore, J. W. (1979). "Select Technological Issues in Agro-Industry." *Social and Economic Studies,* Vol. 28, No. 1, March.

Demas, William G. (1965). *The Economics of Development in Small Countries with Reference to the Caribbean.* Montreal: McGill-Queens.

____. (1988a). "Food Production in the Caribbean Community." *Caribbean Affairs,* Vol. 1, No. 2, pp. 160–91.

____. (1988b). "Perspectives on the Future of the Caribbean in the World Economy." *Caribbean Affairs,* Vol. 1, No. 4, pp. 6–26.

Denison, E. F. (1962). *Sources of Economic Growth and the Alternatives before Us.* New York: Committee for Economic Development.

De Silva, N. T. M. H., and C. A. Tisdell (1988). "Strategies and Administrative Reforms to Meet a Biological Threat to Papua New Guinea's Coffee Industry." *Agricultural Administration and Extension,* Vol. 30, pp. 309–23.

Dodd, D. J. (1982). "Rule-Making and Rule-Enforcement in Plantation Society: The Ideological Development of Criminal Justice in Guyana." *Social and Economic Studies,* Vol. 31, No. 3, September, pp. 1–35.

Dore, R. (1976). *The Diploma Disease: Education, Qualifications, and Development.* London: George Allen and Unwin.

Doulman, D. J. (1989). "A Critical Review of Some Aspects of Fisheries Joint Ventures." In H. Campbell, K. Menz, and G. Waugh (eds.). *Economics of Fishery Management in the Pacific Islands Region.* Canberra. Australian Centre for International Agricultural Research.

Dowty, Alan (1986). "Emigration and Expulsion in the Third World." *Third World Review,* Vol. 8, No. 1, pp. 151–76.

Dupont, Louis (1988). *Les departements francais d'Amerique.* Paris: Editions L'Harmatton.

Dwyer, L. (1986). "Tourism." *Islands/Australia Working Paper No. 86/3,* Canberra: National Centre for Development Studies, Australian National University.

Edwards, G., and C. A. Tisdell (1988). "Comparative Costs and Other Economic Features of Schooling in Zimbabwe." *Journal of Development Alternatives,* Vol. 7, No. 4, pp. 119–36.

Fagerlind, Ingeman, and Lawrence J. Saha (1983). *Education and National Development.* New York: Pergamon Press.

Fairbairn, T. I. J. (1985). *Island Economies: Studies from the South Pacific.* Suva: Institute of Pacific Studies, University of the South Pacific.

Fairbairn, Te'o I. J., and Thomas T. G. Parry (1986). *Multinational Enterprises in the Developing South Pacific Region.* Honolulu: Pacific Islands Development Program, East-West Center.

Fei, J. C. H., and Gustav Ranis (1964). *Development of the Labor Surplus Economy: Theory and Policy.* Homewood, Ill.: Richard D. Brown.

Feinstein, Charles (1986). *Privatization Possibilities among Pacific Island Countries.* Honolulu: Pacific Islands Development Program, East-West Center.

Feketekuty, Geza (1988). *International Trade in Services.* Cambridge, Mass.: Ballinger.

Fiji Visitor's Bureau (1983). *Briefing Notes on Tourism.* Fiji: Ministry of Foreign Affairs and Tourism.

Firth, S. (1986). *New Guinea under the Germans.* Port Moresby, Papua New Guinea: WEB Books.

Fisher, S. (1987). "Economic Development and Crime: Two May Be Associated as an Adaptation to Industrialism in Social Revolution." *American Journal of Economics and Sociology,* Vol. 46, No. 1, September, pp. 17–34.

Fish, E. K. (1985). *The Economic Independence of Kiribati.* Sydney: Pacific Regional Team, Australian Development Assistance Bureau, October.

_____. (1986). "Pacific Island Agriculture." *Islands/Australia Working Paper No. 86/8.* Canberra: National Centre for Development Studies, The Australian National University.

Frank, Andre Gunder (1967). *Capitalism and Underdevelopment in Latin America.* New York: Monthly Review Press.

_____. (1979). *Dependent Accumulation and Underdevelopment.* New York: Monthly Review Press.

Freedman, Sheldon. (1973). "The Effect of the United States Immigration Act of 1965 on the Flow of Skilled Migrants from Less Developed Countries." *World Development,* Vol. 1, No. 8, pp. 39–44.

Ganilau, P. (1974). "Tourism — Servant, Not Master." *News from Fiji,* Vol. 28, No. 13, pp. 67–71.

Garreau. Joel (1981). *The Nine Nations of North America.* New York: Avon Books.

Gilbert, Alan, and Josef Gugler (1981). *Cities, Poverty and Development: Urbanization in the Third World.* New York: Oxford University Press.

Gillis, M., D. H. Perkins, M. Roemer, and D. R. Snodgrass (1983). *Economics of Development.* New York: Norton.

Girling, R. K. (1974). "The Migration of Human Capital from the Third World: The Implications and Some Data on the Jamaican Case." *Social and Economic Studies,* Vol. 23.

Glaser, William A. (1978). *The Brain Drain: Immigration and Return.* Oxford: Pergamon Press.

Greene, James R., and Brent Scowcroft (1984). *Western Interests and U.S. Policy Options in the Caribbean Basin.* Boston: Oelgeschlager, Gunn & Hain.

Hailey, John M. (1987). *Entrepreneurs and Indigenous Business in the Pacific.* Honolulu: Pacific Island Development Program, East-West Center.

Hamnett, Michael P., and Robert C. Kiste (1988). *Issues and Interest Groups in the Pacific Islands.* Study Commissioned by the U.S. Information Agency (mimeo), December.

Harewood, J. (1972). "Changes in the Demand for and the Supply of Labour in the Commonwealth Caribbean." *Social and Economic Studies,* Vol. 21, pp. 44–59.

Harrison, Bennett, and Barry Bluestone (1988). *The Great U-Turn.* New York: Basic Books.

Helleiner, G. K. (1973). "Manufacturing Exports from Less Developed Countries and Multinational Firms." *The Economic Journal,* Vol. 83, No. 329, pp. 21–47.

Hellman, Daryl A. (1980). *The Economics of Crime.* New York: St. Martin's Press.

Herbst, Jeffrey (1988). "Migration Helps Poorest of the Poor." *The Wall Street Journal,* June 15.

Herrman, J. (1989). "Nuclear Issues: The Islands and the Rim." *Pacific Perspective,* Vol. 14, No. 1, pp. 36–46.

Higgins, Benjamin (1983). "From Growth Poles to Systems of Interactions in Space." *Growth and Change,* Vol. 14, No. 4, pp. 2–13.

Holmes, Sir Frank (ed.) (1987). *Economic Adjustment: Policies and Problems.* Washington, D.C.: International Monetary Fund.

Hope, Ronald Kemp (1986a). *Economic Development in the Caribbean.* New York: Praeger.

_____. (1986b). *Urbanization in the Commonwealth Caribbean.* Boulder, Colo.: Westview Press.

Howard, Michael (1987). *Dependence and Development in Barbados, 1945–1965.* Bridgetown: Carib Research & Publications.

Hunter, J. (ed.) (1985). *Papua New Guinea Handbook: Business and Travel Guide,* 11th ed. Sydney: Pacific Publications.

Innis, H. A. (1954). *The Cod Fisheries: The History of an International Economy,* 2nd ed. Toronto: University of Toronto Press.

_____. (1956). *The Fur Trade in Canada: An Introduction to Canadian Economic History,* 2nd ed. Toronto: University of Toronto Press.

Inter-American Development Bank (1987). *Economic and Social Progress in Latin America.* Washington, D.C.

_____. (1989). *Economic and Social Progress in Latin America.* Washington, D.C.

Jackson Report (1988). *Report of the Committee to Review the Australian Overseas Aid Program.* Canberra: Australian Government Publishing Service.

Jeffries, B. E. (1982). "Sagarmatha Natural Park: The Impact of Tourism on the Himalayas." *Ambio,* Vol. 11, pp. 246–51.

Jimenez, E. (1986). "The Public Subsidization of Education and Health in Developing Countries: A Review of Equity and Efficiency." *World Bank Research Observer,* Vol. 1, No. 1, pp. 111–29.

Joint Committee on Foreign Affairs, Defence and Trade of the Parliament of the Commonwealth of Australia (1989). *Australia's Relations with the South Pacific.* Canberra: Australian Government Publishing Service.

Jones, Leroy (1982). *Public Enterprise in Less Developed Countries.* Cambridge: Cambridge University Press.

Kannappan, Subiah (1983). *Emloyment Problems and the Urban Labor Market in Develoing Nations.* Ann Arbor: University of Michigan.

Kemp, Bernard (1987). "Living History of the Caribbean." *Social Science Newsletter,* University of the Virgin Islands, Number 17, November, pp. 316.

Kiste, Robert C., and Richard A. Herr (1985). *The Pacific Islands in the Year 2000.* Manoa: Working Paper Series, Pacific Islands Study Program, Center for Asian and Pacific Studies, University of Hawaii, in collaboration with the Pacific Islands Development Program, East-West Center, Honolulu.

Knight, Franklin (1978). *The Caribbean: Genesis of a Fragmented Nationalism.* London: Oxford University Press.

Lemoine, Maurice (1981). *Sucre Amer: Esclaves aujourd' hui dans les Caraibes.* Paris: Nouvelle Societe des Editions Encre.

Levin, H. M. (1989). "Mapping the Economics of Education: An Introductory Essay." *Educational Researcher,* Vol. 18, No. 4, pp. 13–16, 73.

Levine, Barry B. (1987). *The Caribbean Exodus.* New York: Praeger.

Levy, John M. (1981). *Economic Development Programs for Cities, Counties, and Towns.* New York: Praeger.

____. (1987). "The Limits of Local Economic Development Programs." In David L. McKee and Ricahrd E. Bennett (eds.). *Structural Change in an Urban Industrial Region.* New York: Praeger.

Lewis, Gordon K. (1968). *The Growth of the Modern West Indies.* New York: Monthly Review Press.

Lewis, W. A. (1965). *The Agony of the Eight.* Bridgetown: Barbados Advocate.

Lewis, W. Arthur (1954). "Economic Development with Unlimited Supplies of Labor." *Manchester School,* Vol. 22, May, pp. 139–91.

____. (1961). "Education and Economic Development." *Social and Economic Studies,* Vol. 10.

____. (1980). "The Slowing Down of the Engine of Growth." *American Economic Review,* Vol. 70, No. 4, September, pp. 554–64.

Lilly, C. (1989). "Natural Heritage under Threat." *Pacific Islands Monthly,* March, pp. 34–36.

Lin, V. L., and P. D. Loeb (1980). "An Economic Analysis of Criminal Activities in Mexico." *Journal of Behavioral Economics,* Vol. 9, No. 2, Winter, pp. 25–39.

Linn, Johannes F. (1983). *Cities in the Developing World: Policies for Their Equitable and Efficient Growth.* New York: Oxford University Press (for the World Bank).

Lipton, M. (1975). "Urban Bias and Food Policy in Poor Countries." *Food Policy,* Vol. 1, pp. 41–52.

____. (1977). *Why Poor People Stay Poor: A Study of Urban Bias in World Development*. London: Temple Smith.

Lowenthal, Abraham F. (1982). "The Caribbean." *The Wilson Quarterly,* Vol. VI, No. 2, Spring, pp. 112–41.

Lowenthal, David (1972). *West Indian Societies,* Oxford University Press.

Luksetich, William A., and Michael D. White (1982). *Crime and Public Policy: An Economic Approach.* Boston: Little, Brown.

Machlup, Fritz (1975). *Education and Economic Growth.* New York: New York University Press, 1975.

MacRae, J. (1982). "Underdevelopment and the Economics of Corruption: A Game Theory Approach." *World Development,* Vol. 10, No. 8, pp. 677–87.

Manley, Michael (1975). *The Politics of Change: A Jamaican Testament.* Cambridge, Mass.: Harvard University Press.

____. (1987). *Up the Down Escalator: Development and the International Economy — A Jamaican Case Study.* London: Andre Deutsch.

Martin, L., and A. Panaguriya (1984). "Smuggling, Trade, and Price Disparity, a Crime Theoretic Approach." *Journal of International Economics,* Vol. 17, No. 3/4, November, pp. 201–17.

McKee, David L. (1977). "Facteurs exterieurs et infrastructure des pays en voie de developpement." *Revue Tiers-Monde,* Vol. 18, No. 70, April–June, pp. 293–300.

____. (1983a). "Some Specifics on the Brain Drain from the Andean Region." *International Migration,* Vol. 21, No. 4, pp. 488–99.

____. (1983b). "Some Specifics on the Loss of Professional Personnel from the Commonwealth Caribbean." *International Migration,* Vol. 37, No. 3, pp. 57–76.

____. (1984). "The Role of Service Activities in the World Economy." *Foreign Trade Review,* January–March, pp. 408–17.

____. (1985). "Tourism as a Vehicle for Third World Development." *Foreign Trade Review,* July–September, pp. 163–72.

____. (1986). "Tourism as a Factor in the Planning of Third World Infrastructures." *Foreign Trade Review,* July–September, pp. 150–56.

____. (1987). "On Services and Growth Poles in Advanced Economies." *The Service Industries Journal,* Vol. 7, pp. 165–75.

____. (1988). *Growth, Development, and the Rising Importance of the Service Economy in the Third World*. New York: Praeger.

McKee, David L., and Richard E. Bennett (eds.) (1987). *Structural Change in an Urban Industrial Region*. New York: Praeger.

McKenzie, H. (1986). "The Educational Experiences of Caribbean Women." *Social and Economic Studies*, Vol. 35, No. 3, pp. 65–105.

Meller, Norman (1987). "The Pacific Island Microstates." *Journal of International Affairs*, Vol. 41, No. 1, Summer-Fall, pp. 109–34.

Mishra, R. H. (1982). "Balancing Human Needs and Conservation in Nepal's Royal Chitwan National Park." *Ambio*, Vol. 11, No. 5, pp. 246–51.

Morales, E. (1986). "Coca and Cocaine Economy and Social Change in the Andes of Peru," *Economic Development and Cultural Change*, Vol. 35, No. 1, October, pp. 143–61.

Morales, Julio (1986). *Puerto Rican Poverty and Migration*. New York: Praeger.

Morrison, C. E. (1987). *Asia-Pacific Report: Trends, Issues, Challenges*. Honolulu: East-West Center.

Murphy, T. (1987). "Aspects of High-Level Manpower Forecasting and University Development in Papua New Guinea." *Journal of Developing Areas*, Vol. 15, No. 3, pp. 417–33.

Nicholas, Tracy (1979). *Rastafari: A Way of Life*. Garden City, N.Y.: Anchor Press Doubleday.

North, D. (1989). "The Snake That Ate Guam." *Pacific Islands Monthly*, April/May, pp. 24–25.

North, Douglass C. (1970). "Location Theory and Reigonal Economic Growth." In David L. McKee et al. (eds.). *Regional Economics: Theory and Practice*. New York: The Free Press.

Norton, Dag (1988). "On the Eocnomic Theory of Smuggling." *Economica*, Vol. 55, No. 217, February, pp. 107–18.

Nurkse, Ragnar (1967). *Problems of Capital Formation in Underdeveloped Countries and Patterns of Trade and Development*. New York: Oxford University Press.

O'Grady, Ron (1982). *Tourism in the Third World*. Maryknoll, N.Y.: Orbis Books.

Olson, Mancur, Jr. (1963). "Rapid Growth as a Destabilizing Force," *Journal of Economic History*, Vol. 23, pp. 529–52.

Owens, Joseph (1976). *Dread: The Rastafarians of Jamaica.* London: Heinemann.

Palmer, Ransford W. (1974). "A Decade of West Indian Migration to the United States, 1962–1972: An Economic Analysis." *Social and Economic Studies,* Vol. 23, pp. 571–87.

____. (1979). *Caribbean Dependence on the United States Economy.* New York: Praeger.

____. (1984). *Problems of Development in Beautiful Countries: Perspectives on the Caribbean.* Lanham, Md.: North-South.

Parry, Thomas G. (1973). "The International Firm and National Economic Policy." *The Economic Journal,* Vol. 84, No. 332, pp. 1201–21.

Pastor, Robert (1983). "Migration in the Caribbean Basin: The Need for an Approach as Dynamic as the Phenomenon." In M. M. Kritz (ed.). *U.S. Immigration and Refugee Policy: Global and Domestic Issues.* Lexington, Mass.: D. C. Heath.

____. (1985). *Migration and Development in the Caribbean: The Unexplored Connection.* Boulder, Colo.: Westview Press.

Patterson, Orlando (1970). "Migration in the Caribbean Societies: Socioeconomic and Symbolic Resource." In William H. McNeill and Ruth S. Adams (eds.). *Human Migration Patterns and Policies.* Bloomington: Indiana University Press.

Peach, C. (1968). *West Indian Migration to Britain.* London: Oxford University Press.

Perroux, F. (1950). "Economic Space: Theory and Applications." *Quarterly Journal of Economics,* Vol. 64, pp. 89–104.

____. (1970). "Note on the Concept of Growth Poles." In D. L. McKee et al. (eds.). *Regional Economies: Theory and Practice.* New York: The Free Press.

Philpott, Stuart B. (1973). *West Indian Migration: The Montserrat Case.* London: Athlone Press; New York: Humanities Press.

Portes, Aljandro, and Lauren Benton (1984). "Industrial Development and Labor Absorption: A Reinterpretation." *Population and Development Review,* Vol. 10, No. 4, December, pp. 589–613.

Prebisch, R. (1950). *The Economic Development of Latin America and Its Principal Problems.* United Nations, Lake Success, New York.

Psacharopoulos, G. (1984). "The Contribution of Education to Economic Growth: International Comparisons." In J. W. Kendrick (ed.). *International Comparisons of Productivity and Causes of the Slowdowns.* Cambridge, Mass.: Ballinger.

____. (1981). "Education, Employment, and Inequality in LDCs." *World Development,* Vol. 9, No. 1, pp. 37–54.

____. (1973). *Returns to Education: An International Comparison.* San Francisco: Jossey-Bass.

Ramesar, Marianne (1981). *A Select Bibliography of Publications and Studies Relating to Human Resources in the Commonwealth Caribbean.* Occasional Papers, Human Resources 3, Institute of Social and Economic Research, University of the West Indies, St. Augustine, Trinidad.

Ramsaran, Ramesh F. (1985). *U.S. Investment in Latin America and the Caribbean.* London: Hodder and Stoughton.

Richardson, Bonham (1983). *Caribbean Migrants: Environment and Human Survival on St. Kitts and Nevis.* Knoxville: University of Tennessee Press.

Roberto, Bryan (1978). *Cities of Peasants: The Political Economy of Urbanization in the Third World.* Beverly Hills: Sage.

Robinson, E. A. G. (1963). *Economic Consequences of the Size of Nations.* New York: St. Martin's Press.

Roberts, George W. (1962). "Prospects for Population Growth in the West Indies." *Social and Economic Studies,* Vol. 11, pp. 333–50.

Rose-Ackerman, S. (1975). "The Economics of Corruption," *Journal of Public Economics,* Vol. 4, pp. 187–203.

Roth, Gabriel (1982). *The Private Provision of Public Services in Developing Countries.* New York: Oxford University Press.

Roy, P., and J. Connell (1989). "The Greenhouse Effect. Where Have All the Islands Gone?" *Pacific Islands Monthly,* April/May 1988, pp. 16–21.

Sackey, James A. (1978). "The Migration of High Level Personnel from Guyana: Toward an Alternative Analysis." *Transition* (Guyana), Vol. 1, No. 1, pp. 45–58.

Santos, Milton (1979). *The Shared Space: The Two Circuits of the Urban Economy in Underdeveloped Countries.* New York: Methuen.

Sathiendrakumar, R., and C. A. Tisdell (1985). "Tourism and the Development of the Maldives." *Massey Journal of Asian and Pacific Business,* Vol. 1, No. 1, pp. 27–34.

____. (1987). "Migration and Labour Movement from Traditional Rural Communities: A Study of Maldivian Fishing Villages." A paper presented to 16th Conference of Economists, Surfers Paradise, Queensland, August 23–27.

Schultz, T. W. (1960). "Capital Formation by Education." *Journal of Political Economy,* Vol. 68, pp. 571–83.

____. (1961). "Investment in Human Capital." *American Economic Review,* Vol. 51, pp. 355–74.

Segal, A. (ed.) (1975). *Population Policies in the Caribbean.* Lexington, Mass.: D. C. Heath.

Sethna, R. J. (1979). "Perceptions of Tourism in the Caribbeans." In E. de Kadt (ed.). *Tourism: Passport to Development.* New York: Oxford University Press.

Shelley, Louise I. (1981). *Crime and Modernization: The Impact of Industralization and Urbanization on Crime.* Carbondale, Ill.: Southern Illinois University Press.

Simms, R. (1989). "Malaria: The Killer Returns." *Pacific Islands Monthly,* pp. 17-20.

Singer, H. W. (1950). "The Distribution of Gains from Trade between Investing and Borrowing Countries." *American Economic Review,* Vol. 40, pp. 473-85.

South Pacific Commission (1988). "AIDS in the Pacific." *Pacific Impact,* Vol. 1, No. 1, pp. 9-10.

Spence, M. (1973). "Job Market Signaling." *Quarterly Journal of Economics,* Vol. 87, pp. 335-74.

Thomas, R. M., and T. N. Postlethwaite (1984). *Schooling in the Pacific Islands: Colonies in Transition.* Oxford: Pergamon Press.

Tisdell, C. A. (1975). "The Theory of Optimal City-Sizes: Elementary Speculation about Analysis and Policy." *Urban Studies,* Vol. 12, pp. 61–70.

____. (1983a). "Conserving Living Resources in Third World Countries: Economic and Social Issues." *International Journal of Environmental Studies,* Vol. 22, pp. 11–24.

____. (1983b). "Dissent from Value, Preference, and Choice Theory in Economics." *International Journal of Social Economics,* Vol. 10, No. 2, pp. 32–43.

____. (1984). "The Environment and Tourism in South East Asia and Australia: Experiences and Strategies Relevant to Tourist Development and Administration." *Thai Journal of Development Administration,* Vol. 24, No. 1, pp. 124–42.

____. (1986a). "Conflicts about Living Marine Resources in Southeast Asian and Australian Waters." *Marine Resource Economics,* Vol. 3, No. 1, pp. 89–109.

____. (1986b). *The Economic and Socio-Economic Potential of Giant Clam (Tridacnid) Culture: A Review.* Research Report or Occasional Paper No. 128,

August 1986. Department of Economics University of Newcastle, N.S.W. 2308 Australia.

____. (1987). "Tourism, the Environment and Profit." *Economic Analysis and Policy,* Vol. 17, pp. 13–30.

____. (1989a). "Giant Clams in the Pacific — The Socio-Economic Potential of Developing Technology for Their Mariculture." In A. D. Couper (ed.). *Development and Social Change in the Pacific Islands.* London and New York: Routledge.

____. (1989b). "International Joint Ventures and Technology Transfer: Some Economic Issues with Reference to China." *Discussion Papers in Economics,* No. 6, Department of Economics, University of Queensland, St. Lucia, 4067, Australia.

____. (1990). *Natural Resources, Growth and Development: Economics, Ecology and Resource-Scarcity,* New York: Praeger.

Tisdell, C. A., C. J. Aislabie, and P. J. Stanton (eds.) (1988). *Economics of Tourism: Case Study and Analysis.* Newcastle: University of Newcastle.

Tisdell, C. A., and I. J. Fairbairn (1984). "Subsistence Economies and Unsustainable Development and Trade: Some Simple Theory." *Journal of Development Studies,* Vol. 20, pp. 227–41.

Tisdell, C. A., and T'eo Ian Fairbairn (1983). "Development Problems and Planning in a Resource-poor Pacific Country: The Case of Tuvalu." *Public Administration and Development,* Vol. 3, pp. 3–20.

____. (1984). "Labor Supply Constraints on Industrialization, and Production Deficiencies in Traditional Sharing Societies." *Journal of Economic Development,* Vol. 9, pp. 7–24.

Todaro, Michael P. (1969). "A Model of Labor Migration and Urban Unemployment in Less Developed Countries." *American Economic Review,* Vol. 59, pp. 138–48.

____. (1989). *Economic Development in the Third World,* 4th ed. New York: Longman.

Twyford, P. (1988). "Trade Winds, Toxic Waste Plans Slammed." *Pacific Islands Monthly,* August, p. 48.

United Nations (1971). *The Brain Drain from Five Developing Countries — Cameroon, Columbia, Lebanon, The Philippines, Trinidad and Tobago.* New York: Unitar.

____. (1982). *Transnational Corporations in International Tourism*. New York: United Nations.

United Nations Development Program (UNDP) (1984). *Tourism Master Plan for Western Samoa 1984–1993*. World Tourism Organization, Department of Economic Development, Western Samoa.

United States Department of State (1986). *Proceedings of the Interoceanic Workshop on Sustainable Development and Environmental Management of Small Islands*. U.S. Man and Biosphere Program, Department of State, Washington, D.C.

Varley, R. C. G. (1978). *Tourism in Fiji: Some Economic and Social Problems*. Cardiff: University of Wales Press.

Waite, Charles A. (1988). "Service Sector: Its Importance and Prospects for the Future." In Wray O. Candilis (ed.). *United States Service Industries Handbook*. New York: Praeger.

Walter, Ingo (1985). *Secret Money*. Lexington, Mass.: Lexington Books.

____. (1988). *Global Competitiveness in Financial Services*. Cambridge, Mass.: Ballinger.

Waugh, G. (1986). "The Development of Fisheries in the South Pacific Region with Reference to Fiji, Solomon Islands, Vanuatu, Western Samoa and Tonga." *Islands/Australia Working Paper No. 86/2*. Canberra: National Centre for Development Studies, The Australian National University.

Webb, M. A. (1985). "The Brain Drain and Education Opportunity in Less Developed Countries." *Eastern Economic Journal,* Vol. 11, No. 2, pp. 145–55.

Weckstein, R. S. (1962). "Welfare and Changing Tastes." *The American Economic Review,* Vol. 52, pp. 133–53.

Williams, E. (1970). *From Columbus to Castro: The History of the Caribbean 1492–1969*. London: Andre Deutsch.

Wolfe, B. L., and J. R. Behrman (1984). "Who Is Schooled in Developing Countries? The Roles of Income, Parental Schooling, Sex, Residence, and Family Size." *Economic Education Review,* Vol. 3, No. 3, pp. 231–45.

Wood, R. H., Jr. (1988). "Literacy and Basic Needs Satisfaction in Mexico." *World Development,* Vol. 16, No. 3, pp. 405–17.

World Bank (1985a). *Antigua and Barbuda: Economic Report*. Washington, D.C.: World Bank.

____. (1985b). *Dominica: Priorities and Prospects for Development*. Washington, D.C.: World Bank.

____. (1985c). *Granada: Economic Report*. Washington, D.C.: World Bank.

____. (1985d). *St. Christopher and Nevis: Economic Report*. Washington, D.C.: World Bank.

____. (1985e). *St. Lucia: Economic Performance and Prospects*. Washington, D.C.: World Bank.

____. (1985f). *St. Vincent and the Grenadines: Economic Situation and Selected Development Issues*. Washington, D.C.: World Bank.

____. (1986). *The Bahamas: Economic Report*. Washington, D.C.: World Bank.

____. (1988). *Caribbean Countries: Economic Situation, Regional Issues and Capital Flows*. Washington, D.C.: World Bank.

Worrell, DeLisle (ed.) (1982). *The Economy of Barbados, 1946–1980*. Bridgetown: Central Bank of Barbados.

____. (1987). *Small Island Economies: Structure and Performance in the English-Speaking Caribbean Since 1970*. New York: Praeger.

Worrell, DeLisle, and Compton Bourne (eds.) (1989). *Economic Adjustment Policies for Small Nations*. New York: Praeger.

Index

ABOUT THE AUTHORS

DAVID L. McKEE is Professor of Economics in the Graduate School of Management at Kent State University. He is a specialist in economic development and regional economics. His research has been widely published in professional journals in the United States and abroad. His recent books include *Hostile Takeovers: Issues in Public and Corporate Policy* (edited) (Praeger, 1989); *Growth, Development, and the Service Economy in the Third World* (Praeger, 1988); *Canadian-American Economic Relations: Conflict and Cooperation on a Continental Scale* (edited) (Praeger, 1988); and *Structural Change in an Urban Industrial Region* (coedited with Richard E. Bennett) (Praeger, 1987).

CLEM TISDELL is Professor of Economics and Head of the Department of Economics at the University of Queensland. His research interests lie in the applications of microeconomics to a wide spectrum of social and natural phenomenon in the areas of natural resource economics, public economics, science and technology policy, and development economics. His work has enjoyed a very wide exposure in the international professional literature, and he has served on the editorial boards of eight professional journals. Among his many books are *Natural Resources, Growth and Development: Economics, Ecology and Resource-Scarcity* (Praeger, 1990); *Technological Change, Development, and the Environment: Socio-Economic Perspectives* (edited with P. Maitra); *Weed Control Economics* (with B. Auld and K. Menz); and *Science and Technology Policy: Priorities of Governments*.